FINAL VOYAGE

DISCARD

FINAL VOYAGE
The world's worst maritime disasters

Jonathan Eyers

Rowman & Littlefield Publishers, Inc.
Lanham • Boulder • New York • Toronto • Plymouth, UK

Published by Rowman & Littlefield Publishers, Inc.
A wholly owned subsidary of The Rowman & Littlefield Publishing
Group, Inc.
4501 Forbes Boulevard, Suite 200, Lanham, Maryland 20706
www.rowman.com

ISBN 978-1-4422-2167-3
ebook: 978-1-4422-2168-0

A CIP catalogue record for this book is available from the British
Library.

This book is produced using paper that is made from wood grown in
managed, sustainable forests. It is natural, renewable and recyclable.
The logging and manufacturing processes conform to the
environmental regulations of the country of origin.

Typeset in Sabon by Saxon Graphics Ltd, Derby
Printed and bound in Great Britain by CPI Group (UK) Ltd, Croydon
CR0 4YY

Note: while all reasonable care has been taken in the publication of
this book, the publisher takes no responsibility for the use of the
methods or products described in the book.

For Camilla Eyers

1. Titanic
2. Scilly disaster
3. Tek Sing
4. Sultana
5. Mont Blanc
6. Spanish Armada
7. Principe Umberto
8. Bismarck

9. Scharnhorst
10. Yamato
11. Taiho
12. Toyama Maru
13. Teia Maru
14. Ryusei Maru
15. Tango Maru
16. Lancastria
17. Laconia
18. Junyo Maru
19. Teia Maru
20. Koshu Maru

21. Awa Maru
22. Tsushima Maru
23. Gaetano Donizetti
24. Sinfra
25. Petrella
26. Oria
27. Rigel
28. Cap Arcona
29. Thielbek
30. Deutschland
31. Armenia
32. Teja

33. Totila
34. Steuben
35. Goya
36. Wilhelm Gustloff
37. Kiangya
38. Doña Paz
39. Neptune
40. Le Joola

CONTENTS

INTRODUCTION

In terms of loss of life alone, the sinking of the *Titanic* doesn't even figure as one of the fifty worst maritime disasters of the last three hundred years. Even putting aside an objective and somewhat cold comparison of death tolls, some of the circumstances in which the other vessels sank – and some of the experiences of those who died on, or survived, them – were horrific almost to the point of being unimaginable. They make disaster movies look sanitised, and that includes even the more accurate versions of the *Titanic* story.

The *Titanic* wasn't hopelessly overcrowded with more than 10,000 people, unlike the *Wilhelm Gustloff*. The *Titanic* didn't lose all power and wasn't plunged into darkness when she began to sink, making escape almost impossible for those below decks, unlike *Le Joola*. The *Titanic* wasn't consumed by a swiftly spreading inferno, unlike the *Sultana* and the *Doña Paz*. Those fleeing the *Titanic* weren't shot at, unlike those fleeing the *Thielbek* and the *Cap Arcona*. The *Titanic* didn't capsize before she went down, unlike the *Lancastria* and the *Neptune*. And the *Titanic* took almost three hours to sink, unlike most of the ships in this book.

It is a popular misconception that the *Titanic* disaster had a great impact on maritime safety. The first Safety of Life at Sea (SOLAS) convention in 1914 was a direct response to the disaster, and there have been several others since, in 1929, 1948, 1960 and 1974. Since 1929 the emphasis has been on fire prevention, because fire has been responsible for half of all peacetime casualties at sea. In 1974 a completely new convention was drawn up, which made it a requirement for all passenger ships to be subdivided into watertight compartments to ensure they can stay afloat even with the level of hull damage the *Titanic* suffered. However, as of a few years ago there were still cruise ships in active service that only adhered to the 1948 convention. And most of the disasters in this book have occurred since the first convention.

The *Titanic* disaster continues to hold sway over the public imagination, being the archetypal maritime disaster, possibly because it became a symbol of a dying age, the point at which mankind's belief in its invincibility thanks to technology faltered, before finally being extinguished on the battlefields of Europe a couple of years later. Many of the films made about the *Titanic* use the decks of the ship to represent a microcosm of a society riven by class. Poor European emigrants seeking a better life in America face the same peril as Sir Cosmo Duff Gordon, John Jacob

Astor and Benjamin Guggenheim, some of the richest, most notable men in the Western world at the time.

It is hard to imagine *Le Joola*, the most recent disaster featured in this book, making so few headlines in the West had there been any British aristocrats or rich American industrialists on board. Yet around 2,000 died when *Le Joola* capsized off the coast of Senegal in 2002 and, only a decade later, the disaster is unknown even to those who consider the loss of the *Titanic* – and 1,500 of its passengers – a great tragedy. The *Titanic* has been remembered, commemorated and celebrated for over a century now. This book is about the people who sailed on other ships that met with disaster. Some lived, many died, but all have been almost completely forgotten.

1

IN THE HANDS OF GOD

Catastrophe at sea during the Age of Sail

Life expectancy for the average sailor in the 18th and 19th centuries was unmercifully short. Whilst someone who worked on land could reasonably expect to make it to at least their late thirties or early forties, a sailor could consider himself lucky if he made it out of his twenties.

It should perhaps not be surprising, then, that at times half of all British sailors serving on Royal Navy ships during the Age of Sail were conscripted by press gangs. Sailors were physically overworked in harsh conditions, spending much of the time wet and cold. They were malnourished, eating poorly preserved food; a diet that contained little in the way of fresh fruit or vegetables but plenty in the way of weak alcohol, the only alternative to which was dirty water. They lived in crowded conditions and sanitation was poor. Half of all deaths that occurred at sea were due to disease. During the Napoleonic Wars, for example, 100,000 British sailors perished. Only 1,500 died in battle, whilst 60,000 died from disease, the biggest killer being typhus spread by infected lice.

A graveyard of shipwrecks litters the seabeds of the world's oceans.

Disease and sea battles aside, whether on warships or merchant vessels, life at sea during the Age of Sail carried with it at least a one in ten chance of death. Approximately ten per cent of long voyages met with total disaster. A graveyard of shipwrecks litters the seabeds of the world's oceans, the unknown final resting places of the vessels and crews who never reached their intended destinations, having disappeared without trace – or survivors – en route.

Hundreds of thousands died over the centuries, but death at sea was too commonplace, too routine, to warrant memorialising the loss of yet another 200 crewmen. Two particular disasters stand out, however, because both of them led to the deaths of more people than the sinking of the *Titanic*. One of them – the Scilly Disaster of 1707 – changed the world. The other – the sinking of the *Tek Sing* in 1822 – has been forgotten by all but ghoulish collectors, and the treasure hunters who serve them.

From siege to storm

On 29th September 1707, Admiral Sir Cloudesley Shovell sent word from his flagship HMS *Association* to the other

20 vessels under his command that they were to leave Gibraltar for Portsmouth. They had spent the summer in the Mediterranean, besieging the French port of Toulon as part of a combined force of British, Dutch and Austrian ships. The War of Spanish Succession was in its sixth year, with another seven to go before the alliance of French and Spanish unionists gave up on their attempts to unify the countries under a single Bourbon monarch, which would have shifted the balance of power in Europe away from those who allied against France and Spain.

Shovell's fleet, which comprised 15 ships of the line, four fireships, a sloop and a yacht, had helped destroy eight French vessels at Toulon, but the British-led campaign was ultimately unsuccessful. The victorious French and Spanish ships had inflicted not inconsiderable damage on the ships of Shovell's fleet, and whilst still seaworthy they needed to return to Britain for repairs. Winter would soon make the passage too dangerous, so putting off departure much longer would risk leaving the fleet cut off. Carrying the spoils of war, including thousands of plundered gold and silver coins, the fleet left Gibraltar and sailed into the Atlantic, and a terrible storm.

Squalls plagued the fleet for the entire journey, and when Shovell's ships passed through the Bay of Biscay, gales pushed the fleet off course. It was 21st October before the night skies were clear enough for Shovell's navigators to make an astronomical observation and estimate the fleet's position. They were not where they thought they were. The next day, as the ships passed to the west of Brittany, a new storm brought even worse weather than before. Again, the fleet was blown off course.

At noon on the 22nd, Shovell summoned the captains and navigators of the other ships to the *Association*. Depth soundings taken by his crew had recorded 90 fathoms (just over 500ft, or 150m), which was completely wrong for where they were supposed to be. The only way of determining the fleet's longitude was to use dead reckoning, calculating the current position by factoring in the direction travelled – and the speed travelled at – since the last position was fixed. Notoriously unreliable even in the best of weather conditions, dead reckoning proved to be fatally inaccurate for Shovell's storm-ridden ships.

All but one of the captains and navigators meeting on board the *Association* agreed – the fleet lay off the coast of France, in the latitude of Ushant. The captain of HMS *Lenox* was the sole dissenting voice. He believed the fleet was much closer to the Isles of Scilly, about 100 miles distant from Ushant. The Isles of Scilly were surrounded by one of the most extensive graveyards of shipwrecks in the world (to date, more than 900 ships have struck the rocks and sunk there). This made the waters around the 55 islands some of the most infamously dangerous for shipping. The captain of the *Lenox* believed the fleet would be within sight of them by mid-afternoon.

Notoriously unreliable even in the best of weather conditions, dead reckoning proved to be fatally inaccurate for Shovell's storm-ridden ships.

Shovell ignored him and accepted the prevalent opinion. He sent 17 of the captains back to their ships with orders to be ready to continue at his signal. Three of the ships he ordered to break formation and head for Falmouth instead. One of those ships was the *Lenox*. Listening to Shovell's orders rather than his own inclinations, the captain of the *Lenox* followed a direct north-easterly route toward Cornwall. The three vessels soon found themselves amongst the rocky islets to the southwest of the Isles of Scilly. The *Lenox* managed to evade them, but another of the ships, the fireship HMS *Phoenix*, struck the rocks. Her captain quickly ordered the ship beached, and running her ashore on the sands between Tresco and St Martin's was the only thing that saved her crew from suffering the same fate as many of those on the rest of Shovell's ships.

The Isles of Scilly were surrounded by one of the most extensive graveyards of shipwrecks in the world.

The Scilly Disaster

At 6pm, as the sun set and a fresh storm mounted, its cloudbank blocking out the moonlight, Shovell sent his signal to the rest of the fleet. A light frigate usually led the way, but those were the ships Shovell had dispatched to Falmouth. As night fell, and it became so dark the ships could only see each other – when the weather permitted – by their lights, the *Association* took the lead position.

According to local account, one of the crewmen aboard the *Association* was from the Isles of Scilly. Apparently he smelt burning kelp (a practice that had become something of an industry on the islands in the previous 20 years, the soda ash produced from burning seaweed being used in the production of soap, dyes, glass and gunpowder). Realising the captain of the *Lenox* had been right, and the fleet was nearing the Isles of Scilly, he warned Shovell to change course. In one version of the story, Shovell hanged the man from the yardarm. Regardless, the story is undoubtedly apocryphal, not least because nobody on the *Association* survived to have reported it.

Crewmen on the third-rate ship of the line HMS *Monmouth* were the first to spot the rocks to leeward. The captain of the *Monmouth* ordered evasive manoeuvres and the ship narrowly avoided collision. He didn't have time to warn the rest of the fleet.

The *Association* was only 10 years old. A second-rate ship of the line, she was 165ft (50m) long and had 90 guns (by comparison, fifty years later HMS *Victory* was commissioned with 100). In 1703, whilst anchored off Harwich, the *Association* was caught in the Great Storm that wrecked 13 Royal Navy ships and killed almost 1,500 seamen. Some of the strongest winds ever recorded carried the *Association* almost as far as Sweden. But she survived, going on to assist in the capture of Gibraltar less than nine months later. When she smashed into Outer Gilstone Rock she sank in only three minutes.

Too late, Shovell must have realised his mistake. Before the Association *finally broke apart, three of her guns were fired.*

Too late, Shovell must have realised his mistake. Before the *Association* finally broke apart, three of her guns were fired. The crews of some of the other ships heard and immediately changed course. For some of those ships it was also too late. The captain of HMS *St George* didn't know which way to turn, and when he did, the ship also struck rocks, which caused serious damage to her stern. (The damage didn't prove fatal, and the *St George* did eventually make it to Portsmouth.)

The most westerly part of England is Crim Rocks, which is infamous for the 'tearing ledges' hidden just beneath the surface in the waters all around the islets. Onto these jagged spiked rocks sailed HMS *Eagle*, a 165ft (48m) third-rate ship of the line. The storm dragged the *Eagle* over a mile further north before she finally sank.

Meanwhile other ships in the fleet had lost sight of the lights from the *Association*. Now even the crews who had not heard her gunfire, the sound lost behind the roar of the storm, realised what must have happened, and fired their guns too. This didn't save HMS *Romney*, however. The 130ft (40m) fourth-rate ship of the line hit Bishop Rock and sank not far from where the *Eagle* had gone down only minutes before.

The final ship to founder was the fireship HMS *Firebrand*. Her smaller size made her no more manoeuvrable than the *Association*, and probably more susceptible to the strong storm winds. The *Firebrand* smashed into Outer Gilstone Rock, just like Shovell's flagship before her, but the *Firebrand* struck with such ferocity that she became stuck on the rocks. A large wave eventually lifted her off, but she started sinking fast. With nothing to lose, her captain steered the flooded ship for St Agnes, though of course he had no idea where he was, or where he was going. The *Firebrand* sank just offshore, close to Menglow Rock.

The *Firebrand*'s captain's quick thinking may not have saved the ship, but it saved the lives of 12 of his 40 crew, including his own. As the ship disappeared beneath the tumultuous waves, the captain and six of his men managed to board a small boat, which they used to reach the shallows of St Agnes. Another five men made it to the shore using pieces of floating wooden wreckage from their smashed vessel. As the 12 men later discovered, from the other three ships that sank, they would be joined by only one more survivor.

Legacy of the dead

Shovell's body was discovered on the beaches of St Mary's the next morning. Another local legend claims he was still alive when he reached the shore and that a couple of women murdered him to steal his emerald ring. It is just as likely to be apocryphal as the story of the local crewman aboard the *Association*, and for the same reason. Everyone on board the *Association* drowned, between 800 and 900 men. In better conditions some of the men might have been able to swim to shore, but in the heaving seas of the night before they were quickly overcome.

The storm current had been strong enough to carry Shovell's body to St Mary's, after all, seven miles

In better conditions some of the men might have been able to swim to shore.

from where the *Association* sank. There had never been any real prospect of rescue by the other ships in the fleet. They were too busy saving themselves.

Another 400 to 500 men died after the *Eagle* hit Crim Rocks, and as many again when the *Romney* sank. By almost miraculous luck, one crewman from the *Romney*, a former butcher serving aboard as quartermaster, managed to survive. He was the thirteenth and final survivor of the Scilly Disaster. Whilst the exact number of dead is unknown, the lowest estimate stands at 1,400, and a more realistic figure would be much higher. For days afterwards bodies and wreckage washed up on the beaches of the Isles of Scilly, but most of those who lost their lives were swept out to sea, their remains never found.

For the British government the loss of so many ships and men in one incident represented a double blow, seeing as it followed Shovell's fleet's failure to take Toulon. This was not yet the Royal Navy that ruled the waves

For days afterwards bodies and wreckage washed up on the beaches of the Isles of Scilly.

for Britannia, and the government realised that becoming the dominant naval power in the world wasn't simply a matter of the number of ships or their firepower. The investigation into the disaster concluded that the navigators' inability to work out longitude to a sufficiently accurate degree was the principle cause. Finding a new way of calculating longitude was already of growing importance, especially with the increasing frequency of transatlantic crossings.

The Longitude Act of 1714 established a prize fund of £20,000 (nearly £3 million in today's money) for anyone who could find a way to determine longitude accurately whilst at sea and out of sight of land. Isaac Newton and Edmond Halley (the mathematician and astronomer best known for working out the orbit of the eponymous comet) both attempted to find a solution, but were ultimately unsuccessful.

The problem stemmed from the fact that to work out a precise bearing, navigators needed to know the time at a fixed point. Out of sight of land this became especially difficult, not least because for every 15 degrees a ship travelled east or west, the local time moved either forward or back an hour. What was needed was a timepiece that could keep the time at sea, but unfortunately the most reliable means of keeping time on land was the pendulum clock, and the motion of the sea meant they couldn't work on ships, least of all in the rocky conditions Shovell's fleet experienced.

It wasn't until 1773 that self-trained clockmaker John Harrison claimed the prize (though having already received interim payments from the Board of Longitude, the final sum was much reduced from the initial reward offered). Harrison's chronometer was just a little larger than a pocketwatch, and used a wind-up clockwork mechanism rather than a pendulum to keep track of time. Though it took many years before the chronometer became a standard piece of onboard equipment, by the mid-19th century many captains (let alone ship owners) considered them essential for long distance voyages. Harrison's first four prototypes can be seen on display at the National Maritime Museum, Greenwich. All but one of them continue to run.

Titanic of the East

Meanwhile, on the other side of the world, China was growing rich off the back of ever-increasing British demand for what was becoming one of China's core commodities: tea. In 1793 the Chinese Emperor proclaimed that henceforth only silver would be accepted from foreign merchants who wanted to buy Chinese produce. Buying tea, which only had one use and no intrinsic value, with a precious metal that could then be traded with anyone anywhere, gave the Chinese economy a massive boost, but proved a massive drain on the British economy, especially because the British had insufficient silver, so had to buy it from other countries with gold.

Everything changed when the British East India Company, already so successful with its trading monopolies on the Indian subcontinent, turned the tables on the Chinese. The Company flooded China with opium, which was legal for European merchants to trade, even if it was illegal in China. The Chinese economy suffered on two fronts. Not only was the British East India Company using its opium profits to buy the silver the Chinese demanded for their tea (essentially getting the Chinese to pay for the British to take their tea), but that silver then bled out of the economy as it was used to buy the illicit opium. These events would lead to the First Opium War in 1839, but even by 1822 China's economy was already in free-fall, hardship was widespread, and many sought to leave the country.

The sugar cane fields of Indonesia offered the promise of stable employment to Chinese coolies and others who risked starvation if they stayed in China. Desperate emigrants descended on ports like Amoy (now Xiamen) and crowded onto junks heading for Java. On 14th January 1822, more than 1,600 of them boarded the *Tek Sing*.

At 165ft (50m) long and displacing over 1,000 tons, the *Tek Sing* was one of the largest ocean-going junks operating in the South China Sea. Constructed almost entirely from wood, she had a square bow, a high stern and three masts, the tallest of which was over 90ft (27m) high. Her name meant 'true star'. For her latest voyage she carried a cargo comprising over 350,000 separate pieces of porcelain, from teapots to opium containers and urinals, plus raw silk, bamboo furniture, brass, bronze, mercury and much more besides. She bore so much cargo, in fact, that there wasn't room for all of it in her holds, and some of it was strapped to the outside of her hull.

Merchants, couriers and students joined the 1,600 emigrants and between 200 and 400 crewmen on board. Entire families travelled together, ranging in age from six years old to almost 80. The junk was so overcrowded that most of the passengers spent the voyage outside on deck, where each person had room only for their rolled-out bamboo mat. Everyone on board had to bring enough food to last them the journey, which was expected to take a month.

Three weeks into the voyage, on 6th February, the *Tek Sing*'s captain, Io Tauko, decided to take a shortcut through the Gaspar Strait, going to the west of Belitung Island rather than the usual route, passing it to the east. Tauko was considered an experienced and knowledgeable master, having *Entire families travelled together, ranging in age from six years old to almost 80.* made this journey with the *Tek Sing* numerous times. Why he made the ultimately catastrophic decision to take this shortcut when he knew the dangers of the Belvidere Shoals has been much speculated upon in China since. He may have been trying to escape pirates, or he may simply have been concerned that the supplies of fresh water aboard would run out before reaching Java if he took the longer route to the east of Belitung.

As the *Tek Sing* passed through the Gaspar Strait her crew had to contend with a strong northwesterly monsoon wind, which created a considerable swell on the surface of the sea. This made the foamy crests of the wind-swept waves indistinguishable from those breaking over the reefs of the Belvidere Shoals until it was too late for the crew of the *Tek Sing* to avoid them.

The *Tek Sing* struck the barely hidden reef at such speed that the impact would have felt like an explosion to those on board. The junk's planked hull broke open in much the same way as the *Titanic*'s iron hull split apart at the seams when she struck the iceberg. Water rushed into the *Tek Sing*'s holds, and as she slipped lower and lower into the sea, the rising tide and the monsoon wind dragged her over on to her side. Only an hour after running aground, the *Tek Sing*'s wreck lay 100ft (30m) below the surface, and the stormy waters above were full of debris, cargo, and over a thousand passengers.

> *The* Tek Sing *struck the barely hidden reef at such speed that the impact would have felt like an explosion to those on board.*

Survivors of the 'True Star'

The next day, the British merchant vessel *Indiana* passed the Belvidere Shoals on her way from Batavia (now Jakarta) to Borneo. That her captain, James Pearl, also opted to go through the Gaspar Strait – despite it being the less direct route for him – lends credence to the suggestion that he was smuggling half a million pounds worth of opium into Borneo. When the *Indiana*'s crew first spotted the floating debris from the *Tek Sing* at a distance, they thought what they could see was the reef breaching the surface. But as the *Indiana* drew nearer, the scale of the previous night's disaster became clear.

As Pearl himself put it, the sea was covered with humans for miles all around. Hundreds of survivors were struggling in the water, clinging to pieces of shattered wood that had broken away from the junk as she went down. Every empty box, piece of bamboo furniture, bundle of umbrellas or fragment of hull bore several survivors.

The sea was covered with humans for miles all around.

Some of those the *Indiana* brought aboard later claimed they had survived by standing in the shallow waters washing over the very reef that sank the *Tek Sing*.

Pearl ordered the *Indiana* to hove-to, despite the fact they were dangerously close to the reef themselves. Manning them with his best officers and most able seamen, Pearl lowered the ship's boats and started pulling people from the water. Unfortunately his crew spoke very little Chinese, and the poor Chinese migrants spoke no English, and this mutual incomprehension hampered the *Indiana*'s rescue efforts. In the end he managed to rescue about 190 of the *Tek Sing*'s passengers before continuing on to Borneo.

A further 18 were rescued some distance away by the crew of a wangkang, a type of small Chinese junk, about a quarter the size of the *Tek Sing*. The wangkang's crew discovered all 18 clinging to a large section of one of the *Tek Sing*'s masts that had snapped off as she capsized. When the wangkang set course for port, that sealed the fate of any other survivors still out there. Upwards of 1,600 people who left the port of Amoy aboard the *Tek Sing* would never be accounted for.

In 1999, British professional wreck salvager Michael Hatcher discovered the *Tek Sing* by accident. Divers from his ship, *Restless M*, sent down to investigate a mysterious sonar blip discovered an odd mound on the seabed 100ft

(30.5m) down. It didn't take much excavation before the divers uncovered the almost miraculously preserved contents of the *Tek Sing*'s holds. The subsequent salvage operation brought over 350,000 intact pieces of porcelain up to the surface, along with items dating back to before the 16th century (later theorised to have been antiques brought aboard by passengers). None of the human remains found within the wreck were removed. The following year the *Tek Sing*'s treasures went to auction, and Hatcher allegedly made $30 million from it.

Individual items from the *Tek Sing*'s cargo still regularly come up for auction online, with a porcelain soup spoon recently going for less than £15 and a boy fetish (an ornamental figurine which a woman would hold in one hand, rubbing the spot on its belly with the other, in the hope that fate would favour her with a son rather than a daughter) having an asking price of £850. Indeed, most internet searches for the *Tek Sing* will lead to websites about her treasure. Searches return little information about the vessel or her passengers, despite the catastrophe having been the single deadliest maritime disaster in history up to that point, an undesirable accolade it kept for almost half a century afterwards.

2

AMERICA'S *TITANIC*

Triumph and tragedy aboard the *Sultana*

On Palm Sunday, 9th April 1865, General Robert E Lee received Lieutenant General Ulysses S Grant in the sitting room of a private house in the village of Appomattox Courthouse, Virginia. There, Lee signed the document that agreed the surrender of the Army of North Virginia, the largest component of the Confederate States of America military, which Lee commanded. When Grant, commander of the entire Union army, accepted Lee's signature, the American Civil War effectively came to an end. Pockets of Confederate resistance would continue to fight on, some of them until June, but politically as well as militarily, after four years of bloody conflict, the Union had won.

Five days later, 26-year-old actor John Wilkes Booth took advantage of his celebrity to pass unhindered through Ford's Theatre in Washington DC. Fresh from his victory, Abraham Lincoln was enjoying a performance of *Our American Cousin* when Booth, a Confederate sympathiser, slipped into the balcony box where the President sat and shot him in the back of the head with a small pistol. Lincoln died from his injuries the next morning. Following the assassination, all telegraphic communication between the Union and the Confederacy was cut off. Many in the defeated South did not learn of Lincoln's death until news was brought down the Mississippi River by ships sent to aid in the repatriation of Union prisoners of war newly released from Confederate camps.

Conditions in those overcrowded prisoner of war camps had been notoriously bad throughout the Civil War, but in the final year of the conflict, as events turned against the Confederacy, they had grown even worse. The Confederate armies found it increasingly difficult to provide sufficient food and medicine for their own troops, let alone tens of thousands of prisoners. In the infamous camp at Andersonville, Georgia, 13,000 of the 45,000 prisoners died either of starvation or disease. Many of the prisoners were young (some had been only 14 when captured, having enlisted as musicians rather than soldiers, or lied about their age) and many had been wounded on the battlefield prior to capture. By the time the war ended, many of those who had survived prolonged captivity were reduced to a skeletal state, picking undigested wheat and oats out of animal dung because there was little else to eat.

With most of Mississippi now under direct Union control, army officials negotiated the immediate parole of prisoners of war from camps throughout the Southern states. Over 5,000 men from Andersonville and another camp, Cahaba in Alabama, were brought to Camp Fisk, east of Vicksburg, Mississippi, to await repatriation to the North. The Union officials decided to prioritise the ill and the half-starved for transport aboard Northern steamships that came down the river and docked at Vicksburg.

Despite being weakened by their imprisonment, war injuries, hunger, sickness and sometimes cruel torture, the men were in good spirits.

Despite being weakened by their imprisonment, war injuries, hunger, sickness and sometimes cruel torture, the men who waited on the wharves at Vicksburg were in good spirits. Some had walked for 50 miles without shoes or food to reach Camp Fisk. Many of the men were from Ohio and were desperate to get back home. They would return not as freed prisoners but as heroes, victors revelling in glory. But many of them would never make it. On 12th April 1865, the SS *Sultana* was inspected in St Louis, Missouri, and approved to join the repatriation efforts. When she left St Louis shortly thereafter, it was the beginning of her final voyage.

Warning signs

Constructed in Cincinnati, Ohio in 1863, the *Sultana* was a 1,700-ton wooden paddle wheeler built with the Mississippi cotton trade in mind. Whilst many steam-

powered paddle wheelers operating at the southern end of
the river had stern-mounted wheels, the *Sultana* had side-
mounted wheels, which made her wider (some 42ft, or
12m, at her widest point), but also increased her
manoeuvrability – especially important in the twisting
stretches of the river and its tributaries further north.

As well as carrying cargo, the 260ft (79m) long steamship
had enough berths or cabins for up to 376 people, including
85 crewmen. Twin funnels towered over her three
whitewashed decks. Being such a new ship the *Sultana* had
what was at the time the most modern safety equipment
available, including gauges in the four boilers that locked
open if pressure reached dangerous levels. There were also
fire-fighting pumps, buckets, axes and a hose longer than
the ship herself.

For the *Sultana*'s captain, J Cass Mason, war had been
good for business. In the two years since the ship's launch
he had run back and forth between St Louis and New
Orleans regularly (the Mississippi River having been under
Union control since the successful Siege of Vicksburg in
May–July 1863). The War Department of the Union
frequently commissioned him to
carry troops aboard, which may
have made the *Sultana* a target for
the Confederate armies, but
Mason considered it worth the risk. After all, the War
Department paid him $5 for every enlisted soldier (and
double that for every officer) he transported downriver
towards the frontline. Mason probably wasn't alone
amongst steamship captains in offering military officials a
$1.50 per head rebate (some might have called it a bribe)

For the Sultana*'s captain, J Cass Mason, war had been good for business.*

if they ignored the *Sultana*'s legal capacity limit. Mason often left St Louis with far more than 376 aboard his vessel. The end of the war was going to hit his income hard.

On 19th April, the *Sultana* arrived in New Orleans, where she stayed for two days. When she left on the 21st, she carried about 100 passengers, including merchants taking their livestock to market in St Louis. The *Sultana* had almost made it as far north as Vicksburg when crewmen in the engine room discovered a potentially dangerous problem. One of the boilers had developed a crack, and super-heated steam was escaping. Mason had no choice but to slow down to ease the pressure in the boilers. Though only 10 miles south of Vicksburg at the time, the *Sultana* crawled the rest of the way, docking in early evening on the 23rd.

Whilst his primary concern was to find someone cheap to repair the leak, when Mason went ashore he learnt that another steamship, the *Olive Branch*, had recently left Vicksburg with 700 prisoners of war from Camp Fisk aboard. Another 1,300 had already departed on the *Henry Ames*. Several thousand former prisoners were still waiting at Camp Fisk, and the uncontracted but empty *Pauline Carroll* could probably take most of them. Mason realised he not only needed someone cheap to repair his leak, he needed someone who would do the job fast. He had already been delayed getting in to Vicksburg, and now he stood to lose thousands of dollars to another captain.

The local boilermaker that Mason hired to do the repair job initially refused to do it. He told Mason that the boiler needed replacing completely, which would take up to four days. When Mason insisted a temporary patch over the crack would do, the boilermaker insisted that it wouldn't.

The boilermaker just removed a bulged section of boiler plate and riveted a thin patch over the top.

The boilermaker eventually capitulated after Mason promised the boiler would be replaced as soon as the *Sultana* reached St Louis. The boilermaker just removed a bulged section of boiler plate and riveted a thin patch over the top. The job took him only a day. Mason was still hopeful of being ready on time to take most, if not all, of the remaining prisoners.

According to a former member of the *Sultana*'s crew who had left the steamship in New Orleans only a few days previously, this wasn't the first time Mason cut corners with the maintenance of his vessel. On two previous occasions a damaged boiler had been patched up rather than replaced, once before at Vicksburg, and once at Natchez, further south along the Mississippi. Mason still considered his two-year-old ship new, however much wear she had accrued constantly traversing the river's often rough waters. Perhaps because the *Sultana* hadn't suffered any significant problems from Mason's piecemeal approach to maintenance in the past he thought the same would be true this time too.

Like bees about to swarm

The army officials drawing up the list of men to be transported wanted to split the freed prisoners between the *Sultana* and the *Pauline Carroll*, but Mason was having none of it. He had a longstanding contract with the War Department for transporting troops, he argued, which the captain of the *Pauline Carroll* did not. The *Sultana* also had a proven track record of carrying significant numbers of men, so obviously that would make it fine to overload her on this trip too. Mason even persuaded the officials that rather than draw up a complete list of men before boarding, the former prisoners could simply give their names as they came aboard, thereby saving everyone – but especially Mason himself – precious time. The army officials finally acquiesced to Mason's wishes. Consequently, the precise number of men aboard the *Sultana* when she left Vicksburg is unknown.

The precise number of men aboard the Sultana *when she left Vicksburg is unknown.*

The first to be brought aboard were 398 men from the military hospital in Vicksburg. A brief hospital stay could not make up for years of neglect in the camps, but if the doctors believed the men could survive the trip, they let them go to the *Sultana*. Many of the sickest and weakest had to be carried aboard. Legally, the *Sultana* was now already overloaded. The first trainload of men from Camp Fisk arrived shortly thereafter, bringing 570 men, and two more trains followed. One of them derailed en route, injuring a lot of prisoners, but all except the most seriously hurt continued to the *Sultana*; they had come this far, and nobody wanted to miss their ticket home. The third train reached Vicksburg in late afternoon on the 24th. It carried another 800 men.

Had Mason survived the return journey he would have found himself shortchanged. Because of his insistence that the men only be counted as they boarded rather than a comprehensive list of those he was to carry be drawn up beforehand, the army officials trying to coordinate the operation from the Vicksburg docks missed at least 400 off the final tally, simply by not being present when they arrived.

More men tried to fight or bribe their way aboard, so by the time the *Sultana* left Vicksburg at around 9pm that evening, there were at least 2,400 people on the ship. One survivor described the steamship as looking like a hive of bees about to swarm. Overcrowded by more than six times her legal capacity, the *Sultana* showed signs of struggling to carry this many. After every berth and cabin had been filled, and it was standing room only, the men filled the top deck (called the hurricane deck). Those on the deck below reported to the crew that the ceiling seemed to be sagging under all those stamping feet. Of course, Mason was reluctant to let anybody off, so his solution was to get his crewmen to install stanchions beneath the top deck, buttressing it against the excess weight.

Overcrowded by more than six times her legal capacity, the Sultana showed signs of struggling to carry this many.

As concern spread and word reached the army officials managing the ship's loading, Mason tried to convince them he had carried this many before and that his ship would be fine. The army officials didn't need much convincing. After all, they would receive their per head kickback for ignoring the legal capacity limit. And the men themselves didn't seem to mind being so tightly packed in. This was no worse than the overcrowding most of them had experienced in the prisoner of war camps, and being on board the *Sultana* at least carried with it the promise of being home by the end of the week.

It wasn't just freed prisoners who boarded the *Sultana* at Vicksburg. Private passengers who had booked a cabin in advance joined the throngs of men at the dockside. They included pump-maker and retired army officer Harvey Annis, his wife Ann and their seven-year-old daughter, Isabella. Ann was sufficiently worried about the large number of men being crammed into such a small ship to talk to the *Sultana*'s chief clerk about it. He told her everything would be fine, and otherwise ignored her.

The raging waters of the Mississippi

Warmer weather in the Northern states had started the spring freshet. As the winter receded, the run-off from melting snow and ice poured into the tributaries that fed the Mississippi. The river ran very high, and the *Sultana* would later pass points at which the river had burst its banks, flooding low-lying countryside for miles on either side. Backing away from the wharf at Vicksburg and turning north, the *Sultana* battled against the raging current trying to drive her in the opposite direction. Weighed down by her exceptionally heavy human cargo, the steamship made slow progress into the night.

The first stop Mason made was when the *Sultana* docked briefly at Helena, Arkansas, about 200 miles north of Vicksburg and less than 70 miles south of *The* Sultana *suddenly developed a noticeable list.* Memphis, Tennessee. On shore, someone with a camera thought the extraordinary sight of a steamship so overflowing with men a spectacle worth capturing. Some of those on board the *Sultana* spotted him and word quickly spread amongst those on her hurricane deck. There was a rush to the port side, as hundreds of men tried to squeeze into the shot. Top heavy as she was, the *Sultana* suddenly developed a noticeable list. Realising what had caused it, Mason's crew ordered all the men on the hurricane deck to move back to where they were. As overheard by a survivor, Mason expressed concern for his ship's safety for the first time. With all those men on the hurricane deck she was top heavy, and another mass movement could, if combined with the strong current, cause the ship to capsize (as happened with the *Neptune* in 1993, see chapter eight).

The *Sultana* reached Memphis at about 8pm on the 26th, and stayed until around midnight. Many of the men left the ship, though most did not go far. Others headed into town in search of liquor. On leaving Memphis the *Sultana* headed across the river to Hopefield, Arkansas, where she took on several tons of coal. Some of the men who had gone into Memphis looking for alcohol had

Though they may have cursed themselves for missing the boat then, within a couple of hours they would probably have been counting their blessings.

found rather too much of it, and they came back to the docks only in time to see the steamship leave without them. Though they may have cursed themselves for missing the boat then, within a couple of hours they would probably have been counting their blessings.

At 2am on the 27th, the *Sultana* was about 10 miles north of Memphis. Most of those on board who could find room to sit or lie down were sleeping. Others found it impossible to sleep as the steamship rocked from side to side due to the current and the constant twists and turns of the river. Some of the men whiled away a sleepless night gambling.

As the *Sultana* tilted from port to starboard then back again, the water in her four interconnected boilers spilled from one to the other. When she tilted to starboard the water ran out of the left-most boiler and pooled in the right-most. The left-most boiler continued to be heated, though suddenly dry, so when the *Sultana* tilted to port, the water flooding back in hit these red-hot spots and flash-boiled instantly to steam. This created a sudden surge of pressure every time the ship careened from one side to the other. Mason could have minimised this effect by ensuring the water levels in the boilers were high enough that none of them ever ran empty. But then, he didn't really consider that necessary. He had probably allowed the working steam pressure to exceed safe levels throughout the journey because the extra power was needed to overcome the strong freshet current. As far as he was concerned, the boilers had safety gauges that would lock open if the pressure ever reached dangerous levels.

As the patch burst open, the sudden change in pressure caused the boiler to explode.

For Mason's own sake, the boilermaker in Vicksburg should never have allowed the *Sultana*'s captain to dismiss his professional wisdom. That patch he had riveted to the boiler on the port side could not withstand the excessive pressure. As the patch burst open, the sudden change in pressure caused the boiler to explode. That in turn caused two of the other three boilers to explode. The force of the blast was so big that it threw hundreds of those crowded on the deck 25ft (8m) into the air and into the river.

In the seconds it took to tear through the doomed steamship, the explosion destroyed the pilot house completely. Both funnels crashed down onto the hurricane deck, killing dozens instantly. Many more were killed as splintered timber turned into shrapnel. The blast also caused fatal damage to the *Sultana*'s superstructure. Those upper decks that had already been sagging under the weight of overcrowding finally collapsed. Hundreds of men – those not killed by the explosion, the falling funnels or the shrapnel – fell to their deaths as the ship suddenly opened up beneath them.

The burgeoning inferno

Described by one person on shore as sounding like the roar of a massive earthquake, the explosion woke people as far away as Memphis, and before long eyewitnesses could see the glow of the burgeoning inferno from 10 miles away. The blast had torn a gaping space through the decks above the boilers and ignited several tons of coal, sending it rocketing in every direction. As burning coal fell out of the sky much of it landed back on the wooden steamship. The highly flammable paint that coated much of her upper decks helped the fire spread even faster than the falling coal.

Described by one person on shore as sounding like the roar of a massive earthquake, the explosion woke people as far away as Memphis.

Below decks, hundreds of men never stood a chance of escape. The first they knew of the explosion was when collapsing deck timbers fell on them where they were sleeping. Not all of them were killed outright. Many remained trapped whilst their comrades fled in panic and confusion. For some of those there was no way out either, with much of the ship around the boiler room already impassable, blocked by wreckage that piled in as the decks above imploded. Boiling water continued to spray from ruptured pipes and clouds of superheated steam flooded crowded passageways, scalding men to death in only a few seconds as they tried in vain to fight their way through the darkness.

In their cabin, Harvey Annis and his wife woke the moment the explosion rocked the *Sultana*. As steam started hissing into their cabin Annis realised they needed to get off the ship. He quickly put his lifejacket on and then helped his wife with hers. In his haste he tied it on her incorrectly. Then, taking seven-

There were men lying dead or dying all around, cinders and ash falling like hellish rain, and sheer panic in the faces of everyone they encountered.

year-old Isabella in his arms, he opened the cabin door. They followed the other men rushing to reach the side of the ship. Coming up on deck they were met by a scene of abject horror – men lying dead or dying all around, cinders and ash falling like hellish rain, and sheer panic in the faces of everyone they encountered.

Men were already jumping overboard on both sides of the ship, most of them not even bothering to look for a lifejacket first. Some were screaming in terror. The boys who had lied about their age to enlist now looked like the children they were rather than veterans. As the fire spread so rapidly, the flames creeping across the *Sultana*'s wooden structure with an almost liquid quality, nobody stopped to try and fight it. Those pumps, buckets, axes and that hose were all useless now.

Harvey Annis saw that there were now so many men in the water beside the ship that it was impossible for any more to jump without landing on top of those below. Some climbed down the swinging fenders hanging over the side of the ship. Others swung themselves down on ropes. But there was no room in the water. As the fire spread in their direction, men surged toward the stern, and Annis and his family went with them.

Some of the merchants who had booked passage on board the *Sultana* from New Orleans to St Louis were taking their livestock to market. In the stern were the pens for up to 60 horses and mules. Just as panicked as the humans around them, many of the terrified animals broke free, and began stampeding up and down the deck, trampling anyone who got in the way. Some also jumped over the side, landing on men struggling in the water. The fall killed many of the animals.

Many of the men still on board couldn't swim. In desperation they looked for anything they could use to help them stay afloat. Men wrenched doors off their hinges

Many remained trapped in the burning wreckage.

and threw them overboard before going in after them. Others broke into a cabin, pulled a mattress from the bed and then lowered it over the side. But too many of those already struggling in the water grabbed it. When it sank, they sank with it.

In the last reported sighting of Captain Mason he was on the upper deck, heaving large planks of broken timber over the side, along with wooden barrels that would also float, whilst supposedly shouting to his passengers not to panic.

Within 20 minutes of the explosion the *Sultana*'s entire superstructure was ablaze. Many remained trapped in the burning wreckage, and the fire now made it impossible to rescue any of them, even if the other men had tried to. Many survivors would later claim there had only been time to save themselves as they left their comrades to be burned alive. The fire soon reached the stern, at which point even those who couldn't swim and had no aid to flotation decided to jump.

Survivors of the *Sultana*

Carrying Isabella, Harvey Annis climbed down a rope to the deck below and then waited for Ann to follow them. Now only a short drop to the water, they would jump together. At the last moment Ann discovered her husband hadn't fastened her lifejacket properly, so she stopped to redo it. When she turned back round she saw Harvey and Isabella jump without her. The lifejacket may have saved her life in more ways than one. Still aboard the *Sultana* she watched in horror as her husband and child were swept away by the fierce current. But she didn't have time to break down. Flames forced her to climb over the back of the ship and onto the rudder. When the rudder itself caught fire she had to let go herself, and take her own chances in the raging Mississippi.

The men began to panic, grabbing at each other and hollering for help that wasn't coming. Some prayed for salvation.

Even for those men that could swim, the river was hardly any safer than the conflagrated steamship. The melted ice and snow that had bloated the Mississippi to more than a mile wide north of Memphis left the water barely above freezing. It was so cold that men who had been badly burnt escaping the *Sultana* didn't realise just how terribly their skin had been seared by the flames. Some men also found it impossible to swim in their clothes so stripped off in the water. With no rescue forthcoming, and the powerful current preventing all but the strongest from reaching the riverbanks, many in the water around the ship started to succumb to hypothermia. Realising what was going to happen to them too, those who had jumped in at the last minute began to panic, grabbing at each other and hollering for help that wasn't coming. Some prayed for salvation.

Later that morning, rescuers who came too late for everyone else would find someone clinging to almost every tree for several miles between Memphis and the point where the Sultana *met with disaster.*

Several hundred men made it to the riverbanks, where they grabbed on to the tree branches that hung low over the water. Exhausted, they had only the strength to hold on and await rescue. Later that morning, rescuers who came too late for everyone else would find someone clinging to almost every tree for several miles between Memphis and the point where the *Sultana* met with disaster.

The freshet torrent that swept Harvey and Isabella Annis – as well as countless others – to their deaths overcame plenty of strong swimmers too, but some of them managed to survive. Miraculously a woman with a baby was dragged several miles until they were rescued by a small boat. A mule that had broken free of the pens at the stern of the *Sultana* and died from the fall as it jumped overboard provided one man with a life-saving means of staying afloat. Other survivors reported seeing an uprooted tree being carried downriver with several men clinging to its roots, all of them singing the Star Spangled Banner as they went along.

Whilst many of those who couldn't escape the river's flow drowned, some managed to keep their heads above water for 10 miles or more. A teenage boy reached Memphis, where baffled sentries helped him ashore. There he told them what had happened to the *Sultana*, and putting his story together with the fiery glow they could see in the distance, they raised the alarm and spread the word.

At 3am, an hour after the explosion, the captain of the steamship *Bostonia II* saw the same fiery glow from the other direction as he came down the river toward Memphis. By this time the *Sultana* was drifting helplessly, at the mercy of the current, just like many of her passengers. The *Bostonia II* turned a bend in the river and suddenly her captain realised that glow he'd seen wasn't buildings or woodland on fire. After overtaking the *Sultana* the *Bostonia II*'s captain ordered the crew to weigh anchor, then launched the ship's boat to pick up survivors. It was a dark, moonless night, and the only light his crew had to work with was the orange glare of the fire reflecting off the water. In total the *Bostonia II* pulled only about 100 men from the river.

With word now spreading in Memphis other vessels powered north and joined the rescue efforts before morning, including other steamships, the *Arkansas* and the *Jenny Lind*, as well as the ironclad gunboat USS *Essex*. The side-wheel gunboat USS *Tyler*, which had seen action at the Battle of Shiloh and later the Siege of Vicksburg, also came to help. Her wartime crew had already been discharged, so she was manned by volunteers. But there was some reticence amongst other boat owners, who didn't want to risk launching their vessels in the freshet current at night. Even without them, the other rescuers managed to save 500 people from the water.

Her search for her family was ultimately in vain. Their bodies were never found.

Ann Annis was found hours later floating on a wooden board from the *Sultana*. Cold, exhausted and barely conscious, she supposedly gave the man who pulled her from the water her wedding ring out of gratitude, though that was from his account of the rescue; she had no recollection. After recuperating in hospital in Memphis she spent over a month in the city trying to locate Harvey and Isabella. She had survived being dragged away by the current, after all, so she had every reason to believe they could have survived too. Her search for her family was ultimately in vain. Their bodies were never found.

The *Sultana* stayed afloat for several hours after the explosion. By the time the fire burnt through the outer hull she was only several miles north of Memphis. What still remained of her gutted shell drifted toward the Arkansas side of the Mississippi and sank there, near Mound City, just before dawn.

A nation forgets

According to the US Customs Service the official death toll from the disaster was only 1,547, but that toll was based on the tally taken by the army officials at Vicksburg.

Survivors from the group of 400 men the army officials missed attested to the fact that they weren't on any list, and nor were friends of theirs who had died. With Captain Mason and the rest of the *Sultana*'s senior officers also dead, there was nobody who could confirm just how many had been on board the ship when she left Memphis. The most realistic estimate, therefore, is that about 1,800 perished. That's about the same as the number of men both sides lost at the Battle of Shiloh in 1862, at that point the deadliest battle ever fought on American soil. For months after the disaster, bodies continued to be found downriver, some as far south as Vicksburg.

Of the 500 survivors, up to 300 later died either from their burns or from the effects of exposure in the near-freezing water. Many others never made a full recovery either, and died *Even at the time, the loss of the* Sultana *quickly became a footnote to history.* within a matter of years. Those that survived into the long term numbered very few, and every year most of them reunited in Tennessee on the 27th April. The last reunion was held in 1928, when only four survivors were left.

Even at the time, the loss of the *Sultana* quickly became a footnote to history. News of Abraham Lincoln's assassination had finally spread through the South, and the day after the *Sultana* exploded the biggest story was about his assassin John Wilkes Booth being hunted down and killed. Almost 620,000 Americans died during the Civil War, with the biggest battles in the second half of the war claiming thousands of lives a day. Another 1,800 at the tail end of such bloody conflict just wasn't a significant enough number to warrant special attention. Ironically it was the people of Memphis, who had been the enemy only a week before, who had lived through occupation by the Union army for almost two years by that point, who responded to the tragedy with the most charity. Food, clothing and money was collected for those who had lost everything.

Meanwhile in the North, when they covered it at all, newspapers turned the disaster into a sensational story of Confederate conspiracies, sabotage and revenge against heroes of the victorious Union. Such theories didn't go away. As late as 1888 a St Louis man claimed his former business partner (a Confederate agent during the war) made a deathbed confession to having blown up the *Sultana* by hiding a coal torpedo (an iron casing filled with an explosive powder) amongst the steamship's coal stores. When shovelled into the furnace the coal torpedo would have caused the boiler to explode. But the claimed confession was not taken seriously.

Ultimately nobody was held to account for what happened. Legal charges brought against the army officials who allowed the *Sultana* to become so fatally overcrowded were dropped. The worst punishment given to anyone involved was a military discharge, and even then it was an honourable discharge. Blame for the actual explosion did not fall on Captain Mason or the boilermaker in Vicksburg. The *Sultana*'s second engineer, one of the most senior crewmembers to have escaped the burning ship, claimed that water levels in the boilers were more than sufficiently high enough. He died of his injuries before he and his testimony could be cross-examined.

In 1982, archaeologists excavating under a soybean field a couple of miles inland from the banks of the Mississippi on the Arkansas side discovered a large amount of burnt timber some 30ft (9m) below the ground. When they charted the course of the river in 1865 they found the Mississippi had shifted a couple of miles eastward over the intervening 120 years. There wasn't much left of her or those who went down with her, but they had finally found the last resting place of the SS *Sultana*.

3

THE HALIFAX EXPLOSION

The loss of a ship, the devastation of a city

By the early twentieth century Halifax, Nova Scotia, had become an Atlantic hub, the gateway for trade between North America and Europe. For American ships the port was the last stop on the way to Britain, and for European ships it was the first stop with a direct link over land to every city in Canada and the United States. The railway lines that ended in California on the western side of the continent ended in Halifax on the eastern side. Halifax's harbour was known as one of the world's deepest natural harbours which never froze. Situated in a large protected basin, 5 miles long by 3 miles wide (8km by 5km), and accessible only by an easily defended narrow channel, the harbour made the city important strategically as well as economically.

Halifax had always proved a useful naval base for the British, but during the 1776–83 War of Independence, due to Britain's inability to base any of its ships within firing range of American vessels, Halifax became an essential outpost. It was sufficiently far away and more than sufficiently well defended to make a futile target for the new Continental Navy, yet was close enough for the Royal Navy to use as a safe haven to gather, repair and rearm the fleet, as well as to launch fresh attacks from. In the second war between Britain and her former colonies (1812–15) ships that sailed from Halifax took part in the successful invasion of Washington DC, which resulted in the Capitol building being severely damaged and the White House almost completely destroyed.

As late as 1935 the American military kept a contingency plan updated in case of another war between Britain and the United States. Though the Royal Navy had moved its western Atlantic base of operations to Bermuda after the War of 1812 (and where it remained until the late 1950s), in the event of hostilities breaking out again the American government didn't want to risk Halifax falling back into British hands. The war plan involved bombing Halifax with poison gas and then occupying the city with troops.

In both world wars Halifax served as a waypoint for Atlantic convoys. It was particularly crucial during the early years of the Second World War, after France had fallen and Britain fought on alone against Nazi Germany. Merchant vessels bringing vital supplies from the United

States were a target for German U-boats, so they went via
Halifax. Royal Navy cruisers and destroyers based there
accompanied the vulnerable ships the rest of the way, as
they had during the First World War when Halifax became
a key city for the Allies despite being over 3,000 miles
from the frontline.

By 1917 the population of Halifax had grown to nearly
60,000 because of the city's growing importance. Nearly
all of the 400,000 Canadian troops who travelled to
Europe to fight on the Western
Front passed through Halifax,
and it was soon made a
requirement that every neutral
ship travelling between Britain
and the United States (in both directions) stop at Halifax
for inspection prior to continuing. Submarine nets were
installed outside the harbour to make the city just as
unviable a target for the Germans as it had been for the
Americans a century before. But with record traffic coming
and going, the harbourmasters struggled to keep control.
Collisions in the crowded harbour had become so frequent
that perhaps the Halifax Explosion was inevitable.

Collisions in the crowded harbour had become so frequent that perhaps the Halifax Explosion was inevitable.

The city had already been touched by another maritime
disaster five years before. On 17th April 1912 the *Mackay-
Bennet*, a British-owned ship which repaired undersea
telegraphic cables between Europe and the American
continent, was sent out to the area where the *Titanic* sank.
There her crew pulled about 300 bodies from the water,
including John Jacob Astor's. Some were already in such a
condition that the captain ordered them buried at sea.

Between 150 and 200 were brought back to Halifax, and almost all of them were buried in the city's cemeteries.

A disaster waiting to happen

Despite the name, the SS *Mont Blanc* was actually built in Middlesbrough, which in the latter half of the 19th century was at the heart of northern England's iron and steel industry. The 3,131-ton freighter was one of more than 600 similar steamers constructed by Teesside's notable Dixon brothers over a 50 year period. Launched in 1899, the 320ft (98m) steamer was registered in St Nazaire, France, and before the First World War broke out she carried various types of cargo all over the world. After the outbreak of war the French government bought the *Mont Blanc*. Because she was going to continue crossing the Atlantic, and would be ferrying wartime supplies, two defensive cannons were installed on her decks. They wouldn't provide much defence against U-boats or enemy warships, but they would ward off small-scale privateers hopeful of finding something valuable to the French government aboard.

In her holds she carried 200 tons (some 400,000lb) of TNT, 10 tons of guncotton, 35 tons of benzol and 2,000 tons of picric acid.

In November 1917 the *Mont Blanc* was chartered to carry a particularly dangerous cargo from New York to France. On the 1st December the *Mont Blanc* left New York, her captain Aime Le Medec ordering her helmsman to set course for Halifax, where they would join the next convoy to cross the Atlantic. In her holds she carried 200 tons (some 400,000lb) of TNT. She also carried 10 tons of guncotton, a highly flammable propellant that needed to be kept wet because stored dry it was too dangerous. She also carried 35 tons of benzol, which could be used as fuel or in the production of more TNT. But her main cargo consisted of over 2,000 tons of picric acid, an explosive used in artillery shells that was so sensitive to shock or friction that, like guncotton, it was best to store it wet (though 600 tons of it aboard the *Mont Blanc* was carried dry). It couldn't be stored in metal containers because the metal surface would encourage picrate salts to develop, and the salts could cause a spontaneous detonation.

Despite carrying all of this military-grade explosive material, when the *Mont Blanc* left New York she did not fly the regulation red flag to indicate the nature of her cargo. Le Medec did not want to make his unaccompanied and unprotected vessel a target for any U-boats who might intercept her on the way to Halifax. After all, a French ship carrying explosives was ultimately destined for only one place. The *Mont Blanc* reached Halifax late at night four days later, but as she entered the protected harbour at 8.40am the next morning she still wasn't flying the red flag.

From avoidable to inevitable

Having refuelled with coal at Halifax, the SS *Imo* was cleared to leave harbour at 7.30am on 6th December. The 430ft (131m) Norwegian steamer had been chartered by the Commission for Relief in Belgium, an American organisation led by future US President Herbert Hoover, to carry a cargo of urgently needed aid to Europe. Her captain, Haakon From, had meant to leave for New York to pick up his cargo the previous evening, but after being delayed at the busy wharf awaiting coal he missed his departure window. When night fell, the submarine nets were raised to prevent any U-boats waiting outside the harbour from surreptitiously slipping in under cover of darkness; a suicide mission for their crews, but one which would invariably result in the destruction of many of the vessels moored at Halifax. The *Imo* would now have to wait until the next morning to leave.

The *Mont Blanc* faced the same problem, but coming from the other direction. Delayed in New York whilst her dangerous cargo was carefully loaded and stored in her hold, she reached Halifax too late in the evening of 5th December and the submarine nets were already up. Aime Le Medec and his crew spent a tense night sitting at anchor outside the harbour, fully aware that, were there actually any submarines in the vicinity, then the *Mont Blanc* was a sitting duck. As soon as the submarine nets were opened again the next morning at 7am, the harbourmasters gave the *Mont Blanc* clearance to enter, but Le Medec was delayed one last time by ferries crossing between Halifax and Dartmouth, the town on the opposite side of the channel.

Though cleared to leave at 7.30am, the *Imo* was also delayed by traffic for over an hour, by which time Haakon From was eager to get moving. The *Imo* entered the Narrows, the most restricted stretch of the channel between Halifax and Dartmouth, just after 8.30am, going 7 knots. The speed limit within the harbour was 5 knots, but it's possible that the harbour pilot instructing From and his helmsman wasn't fully aware that the ship had picked up speed so rapidly.

With an empty hold and a narrow beam of 45ft (13.7m) – a length to width ratio unusual for vessels of her size – the *Imo* cut through the water with ease. Without any cargo weighing her down, she rode high in the water. Her rudder and propeller were not even fully submerged below the waterline, making her more difficult to manoeuvre.

The Imo *cut through the water with ease. Without any cargo weighing her down, she rode high in the water.*

However, this was nothing new to the *Imo*'s helmsman, who was used to the ship often doing her own thing. She had three propellers, two of which revolved to the left, leaving only one which revolved to the right. This meant that when going forwards the *Imo* always veered to the left, and when going backwards always veered to the right. Her helmsman had to compensate for these idiosyncrasies at all times.

Due to another ship blocking her way, the *Imo* entered the Narrows on the left hand side, despite harbour regulations insisting all vessels keep to starboard. Once in the channel the *Imo*'s helmsman may have struggled to veer back to the right. In 1917, not least because of how busy the harbour was, ships were still allowed to travel through the Narrows in both directions at the same time, which made it especially important that vessels entering or departing stayed to the correct side. The 125ft (38m) tug *Stella Maris* was towing two barges into harbour as *Imo* started coming out on the wrong side, and the two vessels only narrowly avoided collision. Had the *Imo* hit the *Stella Maris* then the Halifax Explosion would probably never have occurred.

The *Mont Blanc*, now under the command of experienced harbour pilot Francis Mackey, entered the Narrows about a mile behind the *Stella Maris*, going 4 knots. When Mackey spotted the *Imo* at the other end of the channel, and on the wrong side of it, she was still going 7 knots. At their combined speeds, the two steamers would reach each other in only a matter of minutes. Mackey immediately signalled with a blast of the *Mont Blanc*'s horn that the *Imo* should change course. The *Imo* responded with a double blast of her own horn, which signalled that she would not change course.

Sailors on other ships in the harbour gathered on their decks to watch what they assumed was now an imminent collision.

With the two ships getting ever closer, Mackey veered to starboard and then cut the *Mont Blanc*'s engines, hoping the *Imo*'s pilot and helmsman would get the message and follow suit. Again, the *Imo* responded with a double blast of her horn to negate the *Mont Blanc*'s pilot's instructions. Drawn by this increasingly urgent dialogue between the two vessels' horns, sailors on other ships in the harbour gathered on their decks to watch what they assumed was now an imminent collision.

But collision wasn't inevitable just yet. If he had been piloting any other ship – or rather had this one been carrying any other cargo – Mackey could have run the ship aground in the shallows. However, Mackey had supervised the inspection of the *Mont Blanc* before she was allowed into harbour, and he knew how volatile her cargo was. The ship might survive the impact, but the shock could set off the explosives in her hold. Re-engaging the *Mont Blanc*'s engines, Mackey took the only other option left to him – he ordered the helmsman to steer hard to port. Though the *Imo* was bearing down on the *Mont Blanc* fast, perhaps there was still time for the *Mont Blanc* to get out of her way.

And there probably would have been, had the pilot on the *Imo* not then made a fateful decision. He had ordered the engines cut, but the *Imo* had been going so fast that inertia continued to carry her towards the *Mont Blanc*. When the pilot saw the *Mont Blanc* start to turn slowly to port, he believed she would never be able to complete the evasive manoeuvre in time. The *Imo* signalled with three blasts of the horn – she was reversing her engines. The captain and the helmsman of the *Imo* knew their vessel's idiosyncratic ways, but neither of them was in charge. As the *Imo* slowed, her reversing engines swung her bow to the right.

The Imo *struck the* Mont Blanc *on her starboard side with such force that the* Imo*'s bow was buried nearly 9ft (2.7m) into the* Mont Blanc*'s hull.*

Had just the *Mont Blanc* steered to port, or had just the *Imo* reversed its engines, then the collision may have been avoided. Instead, both actions combined to make collision inevitable. The *Imo* struck the *Mont Blanc* on her starboard side with such force that the *Imo*'s bow was buried nearly 9ft (2.7m) into the *Mont Blanc*'s hull.

Inside the *Mont Blanc*'s forward hold, drums of benzol were crushed and burst open, spilling the liquid fuel over the other cargo.

The Halifax Explosion

The *Imo* had struck above the waterline, and whilst the *Mont Blanc* was no longer seaworthy, the damage to her hull was still repairable. In the pilothouse and on deck, the *Mont Blanc*'s officers and crew could only be grateful that the collision had not detonated the ship's cargo instantly.

Then someone on board the *Imo* – perhaps the pilot, perhaps the captain, neither survived to testify – made the second fateful decision of the morning. As those on the *Mont Blanc* surveyed the damage to their vessel, the *Imo*'s engines were restarted. Slowly, she began to reverse. The two interlocked ships started to disengage. In the *Mont Blanc*'s forward hold, unseen by anyone, metal grinded against metal as the *Imo*'s bow retracted from the gash it had torn in the *Mont Blanc*'s hull. It is now believed this generated the sparks that ignited the benzol.

Once the *Imo* had withdrawn completely from the *Mont Blanc*, about ten minutes after the collision, smoke began to pour out of the hole in the *Mont Blanc*'s side. Mackey and Le Medec knew immediately that the benzol in the hold had caught alight. As a thick black cloud of smoke blanketed the ship and towered into the air above her, both the pilot and the captain ordered everyone on board to evacuate.

They would later claim that they thought the *Mont Blanc* could explode at any second. Even as they fled they were not hopeful of making it to safety in time. Thus they defended their decision not to make any attempt to fight the fire before they

A thick black cloud of smoke blanketed the ship and towered into the air above her.

abandoned ship. The fire being oil-based and having already spread as far as it had, they may not have been able to put the fire out anyway. It's possible that nothing short of scuttling the ship and flooding the hold would have extinguished the flames, and doing that quickly was beyond their means. They might only have had time to move the *Mont Blanc* further away from residential areas. Instead they launched the lifeboats and paddled for the nearest shore, at Dartmouth, as fast as they could.

The *Mont Blanc*, meanwhile, drifted in the other direction, toward the Richmond shore. Seeing all the smoke, Horatio Brennan, the captain of the tug *Stella Maris*, swiftly anchored the two barges he had been towing, turned around and sped back towards the stricken steamer to help. The *Stella Maris* passed at least one of the *Mont Blanc*'s lifeboats as she approached. The fleeing crew in the lifeboat tried to shout warnings about the explosive cargo to the tug, but either nobody on board the *Stella Maris* understood their French, or they chose to ignore the dangers. The *Mont Blanc*'s lifeboats continued toward Dartmouth. The *Stella Maris* continued toward the *Mont Blanc*.

Crowds of spectators all along the shoreline started to gather and watch.

A shopkeeper whose Richmond premises faced the harbour saw the burning ship crash into the nearby Pier 6. As flames spread to the wooden pilings he raised the alarm, and within minutes dozens of firemen arrived at the dockside and began to unroll their fire hoses. Meanwhile, crowds of spectators all along the shoreline started to gather and watch. Husbands were on their way to work, wives on their way to the shops, children on their way to school. In houses and on balconies overlooking the harbour more people stopped what they were doing to view the excitement.

The crew of the *Stella Maris* began spraying the *Mont Blanc* with their fire hose. Other boats also came to help.

Left unchallenged this long (almost 20 minutes), the fire had consumed the top deck of the *Mont Blanc* and now raged furiously, flames leaping into the air through the thick black smoke. The heat was so intense that none of those fighting the flames, both from the *Stella Maris* and from the shore, could look directly at the inferno.

What Captain Brennan did next suggests that he and his crew had indeed understood the warnings the *Mont Blanc*'s crew shouted from their lifeboats, and had then decided to try and fight the fire regardless. When their attempts at dousing the flames proved ineffective, Brennan ordered his men to stop and prepare the hawsers instead. The *Stella Maris* was not designed to fight ship fires; she was designed to tow other, bigger vessels in and – more importantly now – out of harbour. That is what they would try to do, if there was still time.

To a limited degree, word had also spread on shore about the nature of the *Mont Blanc*'s cargo. Naval officers who knew the ship sent sailors ashore to warn as many people as they could about the risk of an explosion. One ran into Richmond Station, based at the freight yards less than 750ft (229m) from Pier 6, and told everyone about the munitions ship burning out of control in the harbour. When the sailor ran out again, everyone in the station followed.

But then one stopped. Vincent Coleman, a 45-year-old dispatcher who lived only five streets away with his wife and two-year-old daughter, remembered that a passenger train from St John, New Brunswick, was due any minute. It would stop at North Street Station, which was even closer to Pier 6 than Richmond Station. Coleman turned round and hurried back to his telegraph machine. As quickly as he could he tapped out a message in Morse Code, warning of the *Mont Blanc* and demanding the St John train stop immediately. He then signalled a farewell to the other telegraphers. Whether he expected to lose his life, or whether he simply expected his workplace – let alone his job – to be obliterated, will never be known.

By not running, Vincent Coleman saved over 300 lives. Some 4 miles (6.4km) from downtown Halifax the St John train came to a halt, and behind it all the other incoming trains also stopped. Before the disaster even occurred, word was spreading across Canada that something terrible might be about to happen in Halifax. When all contact with the city suddenly ceased, the telegraph cables having been severed, it didn't take long for the outside world to work out why.

The crew of the *Stella Maris* were still trying to attach the hawsers to the burning ship. The firemen on shore were still trying to douse the flames. The crowds were still continuing to gather all around the harbour. Meanwhile Aime Le Medec, Francis Mackey and the rest of the *Mont Blanc*'s crew had reached the Dartmouth shore. They ran up into the woods and took shelter. All but one of them survived.

The fireball rose over 6,000ft (1,800m) into the air. A dense mushroom cloud of white smoke towered up to 20,000ft (6,000m).

At 9.04am, less than 25 minutes after the collision, the largest man-made explosion in history ripped through Halifax. The fireball rose over 6,000ft (1,800m) into the air. A dense mushroom cloud of white smoke towered up to 20,000ft (6,000m). The *Mont Blanc*'s cargo detonated with a force equivalent to 3 kilotons of TNT, a record the explosion retained until 1945. People felt the shock of the explosion as far away as Cape Breton Island, at the eastern tip of Nova Scotia, some 130 miles (200km) distant. In the town of New Glasgow, 80 miles (130km) from Halifax, homes and other buildings shook like the town had been struck by an earthquake. Ten miles (16km) away, windows in Sackville and Windsor Junction shattered.

A city in ruins

The *Mont Blanc* was completely obliterated within a fraction of a second. The explosion tore her hull and superstructure into superheated iron shards of varying size, which were thrown almost 1,000ft (over 300m) into the air before they started raining down, still white hot, all over Halifax and Dartmouth. Cowering in the woods on the Dartmouth side, one of the *Mont Blanc*'s crew was killed by such falling debris. Later, people would find twisted shrapnel identified as once being part of the ship over 2.5 miles (4km) away. The *Mont Blanc*'s anchor, which weighed *The blast hit them so fast they wouldn't have had time to realise what was happening.* 1,140lb (more than half a ton), landed 2 miles (3.2km) away. The barrel of one of her deck cannons was carried even further, eventually crashing back to earth 3.5 miles (5.6km) from where the ship had exploded.

By the time the *Mont Blanc*'s cargo detonated, hundreds of people – including dozens of firemen – were standing along the shoreline. The blast hit them so fast they wouldn't have had time to realise what was happening. Up to 1,500 people within a mile radius of the explosion died instantly.

Hundreds more, further from the *Mont Blanc*, were blinded, some by the flash of the explosion, others because they had been watching the burning ship from behind glass windows, and the explosion smashed all of the windows in Halifax, spraying those behind them with flying shards.

The shockwave from the explosion travelled at 23 times the speed of sound – over 25,000ft (almost 8,000m) per second. It created a wall of highly compressed hot air that

The blast made stone churches crumble as if they were built of children's building blocks.

smashed through everything in its path, just like after a nuclear blast. The pressure wave destroyed (or left on the verge of collapse) every building across 500 acres adjacent to Pier 6. Nearly 1,630 homes were demolished in a moment, and another 12,000 beyond them severely damaged. The blast made stone churches crumble as if they were built of children's building blocks. It snapped centuries-old trees like twigs, bent iron railings like pipe cleaners and hurled vehicles through the air like toys.

The explosion generated so much heat that it flash-boiled all the water beneath and around the *Mont Blanc*, leaving the harbour floor momentarily exposed. The shockwave pushed a wall of water away from the destroyed ship with such force that when the water reached the shore the wave could have been up to 60ft (18m) above the high water mark. By comparison, the tsunami that hit the Fukushima nuclear power plant after the Japanese earthquake in April 2011 was about 49ft (15m) high. The wave swept several streets inland, finishing off any houses that had survived the initial explosion, washing away debris, and carrying away the dead and dying. The wave swamped Richmond Station, wrecking the building and killing Vincent Coleman. On the shore, firemen who had had their clothes ripped off their bodies by the force of the blast, and the flesh burnt off their arms by the searing heat, now disappeared under a mountain of water. When the flood finally receded back into the harbour basin, it took with it many of the spoils of its devastation.

Both the explosion and the resultant tsunami caused immense damage to many other ships in Halifax harbour. The vessels nearest the *Mont Blanc* were either themselves blown up or swept away by the wave. The tsunami grounded the *Stella Maris* on the Richmond shore after the explosion killed 19 of her crew, including Captain Brennan. Miraculously, five of her crew survived. The other ship that had been involved in the collision, the *Imo*, had been further away when the *Mont Blanc*'s cargo detonated. Everyone on deck or on the bridge at the time of the explosion died. The force of the water carried the ship up onto the Dartmouth shore.

The *St Bernard*, a South American schooner docked at Pier 6, had caught fire when the *Mont Blanc* crashed into the dock. It was completely destroyed by the explosion. Another schooner, the *Lola R*, was also obliterated. The Canadian tug *Sambro* sank. The British cargo ship *Curaca*, docked at Pier 8, was carried across the harbour to sink at Tuft's Cove, north of Dartmouth, with 45 lives lost. The *Ragus*, a Canadian work boat, capsized, whilst the tug *Hilford* was blown clear of the water and ended up on Pier 9, where it had been heading before the explosion to warn of the danger.

Other ships severely damaged but not destroyed included the British cargo ships *Middleham Castle*, *Calonne* and

Picton. The *Middleham Castle* lost her funnel, the *Calonne* lost 36 crew, and the *Picton* was set on fire. The *Picton* also carried an explosive cargo, and had been only 100ft (31m) from the *Mont Blanc* when the French steamer first caught alight. The foreman supervising the *Picton*'s loading ordered all her hatches closed, and he thereby prevented a secondary explosion. However, he, along with over 60 dockers and most of the *Picton*'s crew, did not survive.

Entangled in telegraph wires, hanging out of the windows of houses, some decapitated by flying wreckage, the dead lay undisturbed amongst the ruins of the burning city.

The Canadian minesweeper *Musquash* was also set on fire, and set adrift, as was the Royal Navy escort ship HMS *Knight Templar*. Several submarines moored at Pier 1 broke loose, but their crews suffered only minor injuries.

The disaster had reduced much of Halifax, Richmond and Dartmouth to a devastated wasteland. Entangled in telegraph wires, hanging out of the windows of houses, some decapitated by flying wreckage, the dead lay undisturbed amongst the ruins of the burning city. The 2,000 final death toll for the Halifax Explosion is an estimate. Because of the mass movement of troops, and the unknowable number of sailors and other transient workers in the harbour at the time of the disaster, the true number of fatal casualties will never be known. What is known is that 600 of the dead were under the age of 15. Many of those who gathered along the shore had been children, to whom the spectacle of the burning ship was obviously more exciting than the prospect of school.

The aftermath

The USS *von Steuben*, a captured German passenger liner now serving as a troop transport for the US Army, was heading home to New York after taking 1,223 soldiers to France. She needed to restock her coal supplies at Halifax and was 40 miles (64km) away just after 9am when suddenly buffeted by a strong concussion. Those on board immediately feared the worst, that they were under torpedo attack from a U-boat, or that the ship had hit a mine. But on the bridge her officers saw a column of fire climb into the sky in the distance, followed by an immense plume of white smoke. Realising something catastrophic had happened in Halifax, the *von Steuben* made best speed to the port. The captain of another ship, the cruiser USS *Tacoma*, also saw the explosion and rushed to help.

With untold numbers trapped under the rubble of thousands of ruined buildings, rescuers faced a race against time.

For those who had survived the explosion, the immediate aftermath provided no relief from disaster. With untold numbers trapped under the rubble of thousands of ruined buildings, rescuers faced a race against time, not only because many were grievously injured and would die without urgent assistance, but also because fires threatened to burn out of control across the wreckage of so many wooden houses. The explosion had set fire to hundreds of buildings, but the pressure wave had also caused furnaces, stoves and lamps to break, burst or spill. Winter had only just begun to set in, so everyone's coal cellars were full, stocked up to last through the cold months ahead. The sporadic fires found these sources of fuel and grew and spread, combining into much larger conflagrations.

In Richmond entire streets burned whilst would-be rescuers fought to contain the flames. It didn't help that so many firemen had been killed in the explosion. Firemen from nearby districts struggled to fight fires in unfamiliar areas rendered even more unrecognisable by the devastation, in which fire-fighting equipment and a reliable water supply was no longer available.

Plenty of able-bodied civilians volunteered to help too, but it was only when the military took charge that rescue efforts became co-ordinated and more effective. Halifax looked like a warzone, and thousands of soldiers were trained to maintain calm in the face of such danger and chaos. Medical staff from three Royal Navy ships, HMS *Highflyer*, HMS *Calgarian* and HMS *Knight Templar* (which had been cast adrift by the tsunami), hurried ashore to start treating the injured wherever they found them.

But an hour after the *Mont Blanc* exploded, most rescue efforts came to an abrupt stop. Soldiers clearing rubble and looking for buried survivors in the area around the Wellington Barracks, at the southern end of the Narrows, saw what they thought was smoke rising from the armoury there. Rumours and then panic spread as rapidly as the fire had – a second explosion was imminent. The military commanders who had taken charge of the rescue operation ordered an immediate evacuation. Some ignored the order and kept working, but most fled. At this point, few knew the facts of what had happened aboard the *Mont Blanc*. Many believed the Germans had launched a massive attack in the harbour, and expected a second attack against the weakened city.

The smoke the soldiers saw actually turned out to be just steam. Barracks personnel were pouring water on the hot coals in the furnace as a precaution. The truth took far longer to spread than the panic, and it was noon before the rescue efforts resumed in earnest. At about this time, trains from other parts of Nova Scotia began to arrive at stations that hadn't been destroyed by the explosion. Thanks to Vincent Coleman's message, people outside Halifax knew more about what

Anaesthetic quickly ran low and bandages ran out completely.

had happened than those picking their way through the ruins. Doctors and nurses brought supplies with them on the trains, and when the trains left again, they took wounded survivors with them.

Over 9,000 people had been injured as a result of the explosion, 6,000 of them seriously. The hospitals in Halifax overflowed with casualties. They were understaffed and lacked the resources to handle a disaster on this scale. Anaesthetic quickly ran low and bandages ran out completely. Some people had their wounds wrapped with ripped clothing. Once the morgues were full a makeshift mortuary was set up in the basement of a local school. That too quickly filled up.

As the number of stretchers lined up on the streets outside the hospitals mounted, and hospital staff adopted a triage system to prioritise who to help, medical staff from ships in harbour began setting up aid stations all around the city to take on some of the slack. Meanwhile, some doctors even performed emergency operations on their own kitchen tables. Amputations and eye removals became almost routine. Surgeons ended up working around the clock for several days. When volunteers from the Red Cross and St John's Ambulance arrived to treat the less seriously injured, they helped take some of the burden off the shoulders of Halifax's exhausted doctors and nurses.

That night, to compound a situation that would have been almost unimaginable that morning, a blizzard descended on Halifax. Almost 16 inches (40cm) of snow blanketed the city, which extinguished all the fires, but which seriously hampered the rescue efforts. Whilst some rescuers continued to work through the blizzard, 6,000 people had been left homeless by the explosion, and another 25,000 lacked adequate housing – this constituted roughly half of everyone who lived in Halifax. The homeless looked for somewhere sheltered to spend the night (some huddled inside a damaged train) as those whose houses remained standing used whatever they could (from carpets to paper) to seal their broken windows against the weather.

Temperatures plunged overnight. Many of those trapped who might otherwise have survived had they been found in time succumbed to hypothermia. The next morning, however, a soldier trekking through the snow to search ruined houses found the unlikeliest of survivors. Only 23 months old, Anne Welsh had lost her mother and brother when the force of the explosion destroyed their home. The blast threw Anne under the stove, where she landed in the container of ash beneath it. Still warm, the ashes kept her alive through the freezing night. She was later nicknamed Ashpan Annie, and her survival became one of few good news stories that made it out of Halifax over the coming days.

A new Halifax

Despite major developments in Europe – most notably mid-revolutionary Russia signing an armistice with Germany and withdrawing from the war – events in Halifax became a major news story around the world. From as far away as China and New Zealand, relief agencies sent aid. Even in Germany the story was reported with shock and sympathy.

That contrasted with how Halifax's main local newspaper reported it, stoking nationalist tensions by promoting the theory that the explosion had been a secret German attack deliberately designed to target a civilian population. Public outrage and paranoia led to most people of German descent in the city being arrested and imprisoned. The police even arrested the helmsman of the *Imo* on suspicion of being involved, even though he was Norwegian. However, the over-zealousness of the police probably helped sate the public appetite for revenge, and by being imprisoned (and all ultimately released without charge) Germans in Halifax were at least protected from vigilante mobs.

Aime Le Medec, the *Mont Blanc*'s captain, and Francis Mackey, the harbour pilot in charge of the ship at the time of the collision, both strenuously denied any responsibility, and maintained there had been nothing they could have done to prevent the explosion once the *Imo* had struck the *Mont Blanc*. Both of them were charged with

The rebuilding of Halifax brought much needed regeneration to a city that had lost its industrial heart.

manslaughter, but charges were quickly dropped. In 1919 the Supreme Court of Canada ruled that both the *Mont*

Blanc and the *Imo* were equally responsible for the mistakes that led to the explosion.

The Halifax Relief Commission, formed immediately after the disaster, saw the disaster as an opportunity to improve and modernise what had been an ageing city struggling to keep up with the times. In poorer parts of Richmond, for example, there was a lot of densely packed and overcrowded housing, and some of the roads weren't even paved. The rebuilding of Halifax brought much needed regeneration to a city that had lost its industrial heart – and many of those who worked there – in the explosion. Housing, hospitals and harbour regulations all improved after the disaster. Modern plumbing and access to electricity was brought to all parts of the city.

By the end of January the Halifax Relief Commission had organised the repair of nearly 3,000 houses. Temporary housing for those who needed it most was being constructed so quickly that new apartments were completed at the rate of one an hour. With so many families left bereaved if not homeless, the Halifax Relief Commission became important to almost every community in the city. They handled rehousing, pensions, claims for damages, as well as supplying money, clothes and furniture to the most needy. Only in 1976 was the Commission finally disbanded.

4

WAR AT SEA

From the Spanish Armada to the *Bismarck*

The defeat of the Spanish Armada by an outgunned English fleet in 1588 came to set a pattern for the merciless sea battles that would follow in subsequent centuries. The King of Spain, Philip II, mustered the full might of his empire at its peak to invade England, overthrow Queen Elizabeth I, bring the English back to the Catholic fold, and ensure that Spain would become the dominant naval power in both the Atlantic and the Pacific for generations to come. It would end with less than half of his ships and only a third of his men ever making it back home. England's decisive victory helped generate the idea – which arguably wouldn't be true for another 300 years – that Britannia ruled the waves.

Less than 20 years before, Philip II had secured a stunning naval victory over the Turks at the Battle of Lepanto, and he probably hoped to repeat his success when he sent 151 ships, manned by 8,000 sailors and ferrying nearly 20,000 men, to Gravelines, Flanders, the closest part of his empire to England. There the fleet would pick up an additional 30,000 soldiers and carry them across the Channel to invade England. The Armada was so big that it had taken over two days for every ship to get out of the harbour at Lisbon, Portugal. Though the English sent 200 ships to intercept the Spanish fleet at Gravelines, combined they only had half the firepower of the whole Armada.

Sacrificial vessels were loaded with tar, brimstone, pitch and gunpowder, set on fire and directed towards the enemy.

Yet the English were victorious. They sent several fireships – sacrificial vessels loaded with tar, brimstone, pitch and gunpowder, set on fire and directed towards the enemy – into the midst of the Armada, driving the Spanish ships from their anchorage before the extra 30,000 soldiers could board at Gravelines. As the Spanish scattered, the English ships took advantage of their own greater manoeuvrability and speed to come in on the attack and then get out of the firing line before the ships of the Armada could counterattack. The Spanish wanted to use hand to hand fighting techniques, getting close enough for soldiers to board enemy vessels, which had been so successful for them in the past. The English kept their distance, and in the course of the Battle of Gravelines used up every last piece of ammunition they had brought with them from Plymouth. In the end they were firing lengths of chain at the Armada.

But the English decision to fight a defensive battle worked. The Pope had seen the invasion of Protestant England as a holy crusade, so the Armada carried more priests than it did gunners. Inexperienced infantrymen expecting to march across countryside to arrest Queen Elizabeth found themselves firing guns at fast English ships they could barely see in the distance. The Spanish realised they were losing.

The invasion routed, the Armada began its retreat. With the English in control of the Channel the Spanish fleet would have to go the long way home, up into the North Sea and then around Scotland and Ireland. Though victorious, the English did not want to let the Spanish return home to King Philip, most of his fleet intact and able to try again sometime later. So the English pursued the Armada for over a thousand miles, and it was during their retreat that 20,000 Spaniards lost their lives. Beset by stormy weather, running out of food and water, chased by the relentless English who would not let the Armada either rest or escape, the Spanish numbers dwindled. One ship, the *Girona*, rescued survivors of another lost ship, only for all 1,300 to die – leaving only nine survivors – when the *Girona* also foundered off the Irish coast. Those who made it to shore were hunted down by English soldiers. Few escaped alive.

Up until this point in history, many of the battles between European powers ended not in the annihilation of one side or the other but in the restoration of the status quo, give or take a disputed territory or two. The defeat of the Spanish Armada marked a change in direction that would reach its bloody culmination in the tactics of total war adopted during the world wars. Victory now had to be absolute, with no prospect of recovery and retaliation. Thousands would lose their lives in the Battles of Jutland (1916) and Midway (1942), but even these death tolls would be surpassed by the worst maritime disasters caused by war at sea.

The deadliest sinking of the First World War is not, as commonly thought, that of the RMS *Lusitania*, on which 1,198 lost their lives when the ship was sunk by a U-boat torpedo in May 1915. In June 1916 another U-boat sank the *Principe Umberto*, an Italian transport ship carrying 2,000. Up to 1,750 died. During the Second World War, especially in the latter stages, such death tolls became almost standard.

Birth of a Nazi superweapon

In 1940, the Royal Air Force having won the Battle of Britain, secured control of the British skies and delayed a German invasion, the Kriegsmarine refocused its tactics. Now the aim for much of Hitler's navy was not to seek out enemy vessels and engage them in strategically risky sea battles, but to deliberately target shipping between the United States and the United Kingdom. Cut off Britain's supply lines and Churchill would soon run out of the near endless supply of American munitions that had helped the British keep the Nazis back thus far.

Their armament would include eight 15in (38cm) guns, which could fire 1-ton shells at targets 24 miles (40km) away.

The German warships that would carry out such attacks were already being built as early as 1936, when the British public and their government still wanted to believe that Hitler desired peace, and the few figures who drew attention to his rearmament found themselves at best ignored and at worst ostracised. In July 1936 the first ship in a new class of battleship was laid down, to be launched in February 1939 and be ready to enter service in August 1940, before the Battle of Britain was even lost. The ships in this class would be the largest, heaviest and most powerful warships ever built in Europe, displacing over 50,000 tons at full load. Crewed by over 2,000, they would be 823ft (251m) long, 118ft (36m) across the beam, have a range of over 10,000 miles (16,000km) and a speed in excess of 30 knots. They would be protected by armour nearly 5in (127mm) thick on the main deck and 13in (320mm) around the belt, and their armament would include eight 15in (38cm) guns, which could fire 1-ton shells at targets 24 miles (40km) away. The first ship in this class was named for the chancellor held largely responsible for the unification of Germany in 1871 – Otto von Bismarck.

The Bismarck *only ever took part in a single operation, but in the course of that week-long mission she acquired the reputation that has maintained her infamy to this day.*

The *Bismarck* only ever took part in a single operation, but in the course of that week-long mission she acquired the reputation that has maintained her infamy to this day. Between leaving the port at Gotenhafen (now Gdynia), in occupied Poland, on 19th May 1941 and receiving the final, fatal blow from HMS *Dorsetshire* on the 27th, the *Bismarck* claimed over 5,000 lives. Despite the worst other Royal Navy ships could throw at her during that time, the *Bismarck* kept on going, seemingly unsinkable.

Originally the German naval command intended to keep the *Bismarck* waiting until her sister ship the *Tirpitz* was ready. Together the two battleships would constitute an almost unbeatable, unstoppable force. However, when delays hit the *Tirpitz*'s construction, the Nazi strategists decided it was more important to hit British targets sooner rather than wait until late 1941. When the *Bismarck* left port at 2am she joined the heavy cruiser *Prinz Eugen* and sailed with three destroyers plus a small fleet of minesweepers and supply vessels instead. In addition, four U-boats were placed along the convoy routes between Halifax, Nova Scotia, and Britain, though they would not attack, just report numbers, directions, speeds and the convoys' level of protection. However, a Swedish cruiser spotted the *Bismarck* leaving the Baltic Sea, and soon British code-breakers at Bletchley Park confirmed that an attack was imminent. The Royal Navy sent a fleet to intercept the *Bismarck*, which they did in the Denmark Strait.

Much of the reason why the *Bismarck* was almost peerless as a warship at the time was because her designers had found a way around the problem that had decided the outcome of sea battles since long before the defeat of the Spanish Armada. Evasion was the best form of defence, so warships needed to be fast to escape enemy attack. But at the same time they needed to be well armed to actually win, and heavy firepower slowed ships down. The *Bismarck* managed to be both fast and well armed.

The explosion tore the Hood *in half with such ferocity that the bow kept moving forward for a while.*

Radiomen on the *Prinz Eugen* picked up radio transmissions from heavy cruiser HMS *Suffolk*, so the

Bismarck's commander, Captain Ernst Lindemann, was expecting the battlecruiser, HMS *Hood*, pride of the Royal Navy, as well as six destroyers. During the course of the Battle of Denmark Strait the British came to think of the *Bismarck* as the Nazis' superweapon. Despite three direct hits from HMS *Prince of Wales*, the *Bismarck* barely slowed. Within eight minutes of the first salvoes being fired, the battle ended for the *Hood*. The *Bismarck* may only have hit her with a single shell from her 15-inch guns, but it struck straight through her armoured deck and exploded in her rear ammunition magazine. The explosion tore the *Hood* in half with such ferocity that the bow kept moving forward for a while. What was left of the ship then flooded so quickly that only three of over 1,400 crewmen aboard her survived.

Following this display of the *Bismarck*'s power, the captain of the damaged *Prince of Wales* ceased his attack on the German warship and ordered a retreat. He knew his vessel was no match for the *Bismarck*. When the news of the *Hood*'s sinking reached the Admiralty, the order came back direct from Winston Churchill himself, and it went to every ship in the vicinity: sink the *Bismarck*.

Sinking the *Bismarck*

As dozens of British warships rallied to join the hunt for this Nazi superweapon – which had not only wounded national pride but now presented the biggest threat to Britain's war effort since the previous year's battle for air supremacy – the *Bismarck* herself set course for occupied France for repairs. Despite the impression she had given her opponents in the Denmark Strait, she had suffered some serious damage. As well as a bad oil leak, flooding had caused a 9-degree list to port, and she also dipped 3 degrees toward the bow. No longer able to reach 30 knots, but still able to outrun many British ships, it would take her until 27th May to reach the protection of U-boats and Luftwaffe planes. Before they could even attempt to destroy her, the British needed to slow her down and make sure she didn't reach safety in time.

The aircraft carrier HMS *Ark Royal* was closest to her, about 60 miles (97km) away. Fairey Swordfish torpedo bombers raced through terrible weather conditions – so bad that they first attacked the HMS *Sheffield* by mistake – to reach the *Bismarck*. The German ship managed to evade many of the torpedoes, sometimes firing shells into the sea to create a wall of water in front of low-flying planes. Others hit but barely caused any damage to her armour. Caught in a gale, she was riding 60ft (18m) waves; huge seas that would have thrown some of the torpedoes off course anyway.

The German ship managed to evade many of the torpedoes, sometimes firing shells into the sea to create a wall of water in front of low-flying planes.

British success ultimately came down to luck rather than superior firepower. The torpedo that finally snared the *Bismarck* hit her rudder but did not explode. Instead it damaged the rudder to the extent where it could no longer be disengaged. Jamming the *Bismarck*'s steering gear, the torpedo rendered the ship unmanoeuvrable. She could still maintain her high speed and outrun her approaching enemies, let alone outgun them, but she was now trapped in a permanent circular course, turning perpetually 12 degrees to port. By the time Captain Lindemann may have been ready to consider using explosives to destroy the rudder, it was too late. The Royal Navy was closing in, and the *Bismarck* no longer had the *Prinz Eugen* to offer any protection.

On an entirely predictable and unchangeable course, the *Bismarck* proved quite an easy target for the battleships HMS *King George V* and HMS *Rodney*, as well as the heavy cruisers HMS *Norfolk* and HMS *Dorsetshire*. The *Bismarck* fired back, making HMS *Sheffield* retreat from the fight, but the other vessels hounded her through the night and into the next morning. Illuminated by star shells to make it even easier to see her in the dark, the *Bismarck* received hundreds of direct hits from many of over 700 shells the British warships fired at her. By morning she could no longer fire back, all of her turrets destroyed, so the British moved in to finish her off at close range.

He saw a man on deck waving semaphore flags to surrender, and a Morse code message flash to convey the same.

Aboard the *Bismarck*, Admiral Gunther Lutjens, who was in overall command of the mission, sent a message through to naval command that the ship would be destroyed before he would surrender. However, as the British turned the *Bismarck* into a wreck, burning from end to end, listing 20 degrees to port and settling by the stern, a British sailor on the *Rodney* claimed he saw the black flag raised – the naval sign to cease hostilities and begin talking. He also claimed he saw a man on deck waving semaphore flags to surrender, and a Morse code message flash to convey the same. Another sailor on the *Dorsetshire* corroborated the report of the Morse message. It is entirely possible that crewmen on board the *Bismarck* wished to surrender, even if their commanders didn't. The British ships did not call off the attack. Not only had Churchill ordered the ship be sunk, but the very conventions of war at sea required the national flag to be lowered to indicate surrender. Nobody on the *Bismarck* did this. Nor were men seen abandoning ship, another indicator that could induce captains to assume capitulation.

Torpedoes fired from the *Dorsetshire* – first into the starboard side, then into the port – probably landed the fatal blows. Soon afterwards the Nazi superweapon capsized, sinking rapidly by the stern and disappearing beneath the waves completely within 15 minutes. The *Dorsetshire* and a destroyer came to the aid of hundreds of survivors in the water, but when lookouts reported what they believed to be a U-boat, the rescue was abandoned and the British ships left the scene. Just over 100 had been saved, and another five would be picked up by German vessels in the next couple of hours, but about 2,200 went down with the *Bismarck*. For the British, their winning this greatest prize from the Kriegsmarine helped bolster national confidence. However, as survivors from the *Bismarck* later revealed, it might not have been the British who sank her.

Secrets of the deep

The *Bismarck* sank to a depth of 17,500ft (almost 4,800m) – over three miles (4.8km) down. Her wreck ploughed down the side of an underwater mountain for the last mile, coming to a rest before reaching the very bottom. Here she was found in 1989 by Robert Ballard, the undersea archaeologist who had discovered the *Titanic*'s wreck four years previously. Her hull remained surprisingly intact for a ship supposedly sunk by torpedoes, lacking even the damage Ballard had discovered on the *Titanic*'s hull. Others who visited the wreck also began to believe the half-century old claims

The Bismarck*'s first officer ordered the crew in the engine room to open all the watertight doors throughout the ship and prepare scuttling charges.*

that the *Bismarck* hadn't been sunk by the British, but that she had been scuttled by her crew.

According to some of the survivors, the *Bismarck*'s first officer came to them below decks in the middle of the ship's final battle and ordered them to prepare to abandon ship. He then ordered the crew in the engine room to open all the watertight doors throughout the ship and prepare scuttling charges. Some of the survivors even claimed to have been involved in setting the charges themselves, intending to damage weaker parts of the keel and allow the vessel to flood. These were apparently detonated half an hour before the *Bismarck* finally sank, before the *Dorsetshire*'s last torpedoes struck. Whether this caused the sinking or simply made the inevitable happen sooner is debatable, but the Admiralty took the claims seriously enough in 1941 to acknowledge in its report of the sinking that scuttling charges may have helped. Of course, that wouldn't have had the same propaganda effect as the decisive victory which was reported.

Robert Ballard found holes in the *Bismarck*'s hull, but they were mostly above the waterline, and he posited that the rest of them weren't severe enough to have sunk the ship, even if she was taking on water through all of them.

Meanwhile, dents in her armour showed that many shells and torpedoes had exploded against her hull rather than penetrated it. Most importantly, there was no sign of any implosions inside the ship. The *Titanic* sank as soon as the two separated pieces of the ship filled with sufficient water to drag her down. However, she was not completely flooded, and as she sank deeper and deeper, air pockets inside the hull were crushed by the rising water pressure. These implosions shattered the *Titanic*'s hull in several places. That the *Bismarck*'s hull was not shattered in such a way suggests there were no air pockets – that she was completely flooded before she went down.

Some of the survivors claimed it was an unspoken requirement that Kriegsmarine commanders should sink their ships rather than let them fall into enemy hands.

From studying the damage she received from the British ships, Ballard theorised the *Bismarck* could have stayed afloat for another day. In this time the Royal Navy could have easily captured the vessel. Some of the survivors claimed it was an unspoken requirement that Kriegsmarine commanders should sink their ships rather than let them fall into enemy hands. For the *Bismarck*, they would have had every reason to. With an identical design – and identical weaknesses – the *Bismarck* would have provided the Royal Navy with unprecedented intelligence regarding her sister ship, the *Tirpitz*. The Germans were going to lose the *Bismarck* anyway. At least this way they would lose her in a way that would protect the *Tirpitz*.

The *Tirpitz* was herself destroyed by RAF Lancaster bombers in 1944, by which time Germany was losing the war on land and in the air as well as at sea. After the sinking of the *Bismarck* the Nazis refocused their tactics once again, this time toward a greater use of U-boats, both for offensive as well as defensive purposes. But the era of the mighty warship was not over just yet.

The unsinkable *Scharnhorst*

Popularly known as *Lucky Scharnhorst* in Nazi Germany, the 772ft (235m) battlecruiser earned the same infamy in service that the *Bismarck* only received in retrospect. Also laid down in 1936, the *Scharnhorst* was just as fast – if not faster – than the *Bismarck*, even if she wasn't quite as imposing. Displacing up to 38,100 tons, her main armament consisted of nine 11-inch guns and six torpedo tubes. She also had thicker armour around the belt (14 inches, or 350mm), which helped her survive numerous direct hits from torpedoes and bombs, as well as encounters with mines, and helped generate her reputation as being unsinkable.

During the early years of the Second World War the *Scharnhorst* and her sister ship, the *Gneisenau*, operated together, raiding British merchant ships in the Atlantic and in 1940 providing distant cover for land operations during the German invasion of Denmark and Norway – basically keeping the Royal Navy busy at sea where the British ships

The Scharnhorst *landed one of the longest range direct hits in the history of war at sea when one of her shells hit the* Glorious *from 15 miles (24km) away.*

couldn't interfere with the landing of Wehrmacht troops. It was in the aftermath of Germany's victory in Norway that the *Scharnhorst* scored her greatest success and secured her reputation as being a fearsome opponent.

The British aircraft carrier HMS *Glorious* had come to Norway in April 1940 to provide air support for British, French and Polish troops coming to defend Norway. In June 1940 she returned to provide air support for their evacuation. The *Scharnhorst* and *Gneisenau* stalked her through the Norwegian Sea, then despite her being accompanied by two destroyers, HMS *Ardent* and HMS *Acasta*, began their attack. In the space of two hours, the *Scharnhorst* and *Gneisenau* managed to sink all three. The *Scharnhorst* landed one of the longest range direct hits in the history of war at sea when one of her shells hit the *Glorious* from 15 miles (24km) away. The several dozen crewmen who escaped the *Glorious*, and the lone survivors from both the *Ardent* and *Acasta*, lived to report being attacked by a warship that could have a 46ft (14m) hole torn in her hull by a torpedo, but which still managed to sink all of her opponents.

Whilst the *Gneisenau* was taken out of service in 1942, the *Scharnhorst* continued to menace British shipping until the end of 1943. By December, an invasion of Britain was looking even less possible than it had after the Battle of Britain. Germany's invasion of the Soviet Union, which had been unstoppable to begin with, was long over, Hitler's war on the eastern front now consisting only of retreat after retreat. Whilst earlier in the war the *Scharnhorst*'s mission had been to disrupt supply lines between America and Britain, when she returned to Norway in 1943 she was on an urgent mission to target convoys from Britain to Russia. British code-breakers at Bletchley Park had broken the Germans' Enigma code so they knew where the *Scharnhorst* was going before she got there, and the Royal Navy decided to set a trap.

By now knowing how formidable the *Scharnhorst* was, the British dispatched a small fleet to the Arctic waters off Norway's North Cape, which included several ships from the Norwegian navy. The *Scharnhorst* could still outgun all but one of the ships sent to sink her, however, and it would take their combined efforts to destroy her. On Christmas Day, the *Scharnhorst* received orders to proceed with the attack on the convoy, but that far north – with less than two hours of full daylight during winter – and in a raging storm, the Germans couldn't find any of the ships. This was, of course, because the British had changed the convoy's route whilst their own warships slowly surrounded the *Scharnhorst* and the destroyers in her company. When the destroyers separated from the battlecruiser to search a wider area, the British began to move in. Listening in on the *Scharnhorst*'s radio messages the Royal Navy even knew enough about her movements, and those of her escorts, to block any escape routes.

Early the next day, the Battle of the North Cape began. HMS *Belfast* and HMS *Norfolk* opened fire from almost seven miles (11km) away, probably catching the *Scharnhorst*'s commanders by surprise. Her forward radar was knocked out, a fateful blow that would hamper the *Scharnhorst*'s ability to detect her opponents' positions. But she started to fight back almost immediately, her captain confident in her ability to outrun any enemies if they needed to withdraw. The *Scharnhorst* shelled her attackers, disabling the *Norfolk*'s radar too. When the *Norfolk* and HMS *Sheffield* – both of which had also been involved in the hunt for the *Bismarck* – retreated, HMS *Duke of York* moved in. The battleship was the only vessel involved who more than matched the *Scharnhorst*. Along with the *Belfast*, HMS *Jamaica*, HMS *Savage*, HMS *Saumarez* and others, the *Duke of York* pounded the *Scharnhorst* with shells and torpedoes.

It took the better part of 11 hours for all these warships to defeat the lone German battlecruiser. The *Scharnhorst* fought valiantly, taking out the *Duke of York*'s radar and inflicting serious but repairable damage to several other ships. But ultimately she was severely outnumbered, and hits first to a boiler room and later to her propeller shaft slowed the *Scharnhorst* from her maximum speed in excess of 30 knots to about 12, essentially crippling her. The Royal Navy fleet moved in for the kill.

As she went down by the bow, her propellers still slowly turning as her stern lifted out of the water, the order was given to abandon ship.

Repeated torpedo strikes caused the *Scharnhorst* to list to starboard. She also settled deeper and deeper into the water. As she went down by the bow, her propellers still slowly turning as her stern lifted out of the water, the order was given to abandon ship. She sank at 7.45pm. The more distant British ships only knew of their victory when the fires that had lit up the blazing *Scharnhorst* moments before vanished. An explosion in the magazine below her forward turrets caused the bow to separate as the *Scharnhorst* sank, and her wreck landed on the seabed upside down 950ft (290m) below the surface.

Only 36 men were saved out of a crew of nearly 2,000. They would only survive a few minutes in the Arctic seas, so a couple of ships quickly moved in, scramble nets cast over the side for men to climb up. Searchlights used to find survivors in the pitch black found plenty of men floating face down in the water. Within minutes the rescue ships stopped all rescue efforts and departed, leaving those still crying for help to a quick and inevitable death. The Royal Navy may have claimed U-boats were operating in the area, but by the time the Nazi propaganda machine had digested the story the abandonment was a callous act of revenge or psychological warfare. Of course, after sinking the *Glorious*, *Acasta* and *Ardent* none of the 40-odd survivors had been rescued by the *Scharnhorst* or *Gneisenau*, who had left more than 1,500 to die.

Without the *Scharnhorst*, which had been the Kriegsmarine's most powerful warship in Norwegian waters, the supply route between Britain and the Soviet Union was now more secure than it had ever been. From the Nazis' perspective, this was a bitter blow. The war in western Europe may have been at effective stalemate for years, but the loss of the *Scharnhorst* was the kind of defeat that signalled the tide turning against Germany.

As it turned out, this was one of the last major sea battles where the outcome was decided by the firepower of the ships involved.

For those allied against Hitler, victory in the Battle of the North Cape was a brilliant propaganda coup, but it revealed significant shortcomings in the way the Royal Navy had waged war at sea for centuries, not least because it had taken so many ships to win the fight against just one. As it turned out, this was one of the last major sea battles where the outcome was decided by the firepower of the ships involved. Soon artillery shells would become almost as anachronistic as cannonballs, and in future aircraft carriers would become the core unit for waging war at sea.

War in the Pacific

How aircraft carriers became essential to winning sea battles is no better proved than by the sinking of the Japanese battleship *Yamato* in April 1945. Despite being one of only two ships in the heaviest, most powerfully armed class of battleship ever constructed in the history of war at sea, without air support she proved an even easier target for the US Navy's aircraft carriers than the *Scharnhorst* had for the Royal Navy.

The *Yamato* was laid down in 1937. Launched in 1940 she displaced an incredible 72,800 tons at full load. She was so big (to the extent that her corridors had directions for those who got lost) that crewmen reported that being on board the 840ft (256m) warship felt no different than being on land – she seemed impervious to the pitch and roll of the sea, which certainly contributed to this general impression that she was not just another big battleship. Vessels of her size and power had actually been banned by

She would fight until destroyed, even running herself aground so that she couldn't be sunk, and keep on firing until she had not a single shell left.

an international treaty in 1934, so the world did not discover just how powerful the *Yamato* had been until the true extent of Japan's military might was revealed after the war. The *Yamato* had nine 18-inch guns, each of them almost 70ft (21m) long, which could fire shells up to 26 miles (42km). These constituted the most powerful guns ever installed on a warship. As it turned out she only ever hit other ships with them on one occasion, at the Battle of Leyte Gulf in October 1944. As with her sister ship, the *Musashi*, the *Yamato* was so big and had such a high fuel consumption that she spent much of the war in base.

On 1st April 1945, American forces invaded Okinawa, the first step in the invasion of the Japanese mainland. Japan sent kamikaze pilots to repel the invaders, and they sent the *Yamato* on a similar one-way mission too. She would fight until destroyed, even running herself aground so that she couldn't be sunk, and keep on firing until she had not a single shell left. She never reached Okinawa, nearly 280 bomber and torpedo-bomber planes from American aircraft carriers intercepting her and other Japanese ships on the suicide mission whilst they were still in waters north of the island.

After surviving torpedoes and bombings in December 1943 and October 1944 (both times taking on over 3,000 tons of water but not sinking), the Japanese navy were confident in her ability to stay afloat under heavy attack. She stayed afloat for about six hours, but even with 150 anti-aircraft guns the *Yamato* was *The water rushed in at such speed that it created a rise in air pressure within the ship, which felt almost like wind blowing through the corridors.* no match for that number of American planes. As explosions set the ship on fire her commanders flooded compartment after compartment, even killing several hundred crewmen in the starboard engine room who were given no warning.

By the time alarms sounded on the bridge, warning the commanders of fire in the forward battery magazine, they had already lost control of their ability to flood any more compartments. Soon it was simply a matter of whether fire and explosion or flooding would sink the *Yamato* first. The water rushed in at such speed that it created a rise in air pressure within the ship, which felt almost like wind blowing through the corridors. Men trying to escape found the water rising too quickly. Those already in the water were sucked back towards the ship as she capsized, her immense 16ft (5m) propellers creating massive whirlpools.

When the magazine in the bow exploded it created a mushroom cloud so big (towering nearly 4 miles, or 6km, into the sky) that people saw it on Kyushu, 100 miles (160km) away. Of the nearly 3,000 who had joined the *Yamato*'s final mission, only 269 were pulled from the cold, oil-coated waters by the crew of destroyers, several hours later. That represents the single largest loss involving a warship in history. Though five ships in the *Yamato* class had been planned, the Japanese only built three, and even as the third was constructed they realised the shift taking place in marine warfare strategy, so converted her to an aircraft carrier instead.

Of all the countries that could have been considered a naval power at some stage in their history, Japan has suffered the greatest losses from waging war at sea. An island nation but an imperial power, Japanese primacy in the western Pacific rested on ruling the waves, in much the same way as it did for Britain on the other side of the world. But such dependence on maritime supremacy provided Japan's enemies with a vulnerability. During the Second World War the United States quickly learnt the lesson the Germans had learnt after losing the *Bismarck*, and realised submarines were the key to defeating Japan, whose attack on Pearl Harbor in 1941 meant the United States could not match Japan with warships alone.

One of the most successful submarine attacks in the Pacific war was by the USS *Albacore* on the Japanese aircraft carrier *Taiho* in June 1944. Aircraft carriers may have held the advantage over warships, but stealthy submarines would win the war at sea, even if they could not then win it on land.

The blast tore the hull open, blowing out the sides of the ship.

A single torpedo from the *Albacore* struck the *Taiho* and fractured her aviation fuel tanks. As a dangerous cocktail of seawater, gasoline for the ship and fuel for the aircraft mixed below decks, the crew's efforts to pump it out failed. Flammable fumes filled every deck of the ship. When the fuel ignited, the explosion was so powerful that those on the bridge saw the flight deck lurch upwards. The blast tore the hull open, blowing out the sides of the ship. Settling fast in the water, listing to port, she eventually sank by the stern, killing 1,650 of the nearly 2,200 aboard. The best defence her aircraft had been able to provide was when one of the pilots spotted another torpedo's wake and crashed his plane into it before it hit the *Taiho*.

American submarines were lethally efficient weapons, but sometimes too efficient, with indiscriminate targeting of enemy vessels. In the last year of the Second World War, as Japanese forces retreated and regrouped, American submarines tried to prevent mass troop movements between Pacific islands and killed tens of thousands crammed on to troopships. The USS *Sturgeon* scored the deadliest single strike, her torpedo attack causing the

Toyama Maru's fuel tanks to explode. As the ship turned into an inferno, 5,400 Japanese soldiers died. Only 600 survived. The deadliest single submarine was the USS *Rasher*, which in 1944 alone killed 2,665 aboard the *Teia Maru* and 4,998 aboard the *Ryusei Maru*. However, this indiscriminate targeting – compounded by an inability to know exactly what was aboard the enemy vessels – led the *Rasher* to sink another Japanese ship on the same day it sank the *Ryusei Maru*, the *Tango Maru*. But instead of troops, this ship carried hundreds of Allied prisoners of war and thousands of Indonesian slave labourers. This was not an isolated incident, but the submarine crews would not know the number and scale of these friendly fire disasters until after the war (see chapter six).

5 BRITAIN'S DARKEST HOUR

The loss of the *Lancastria* and why Churchill covered it up

As retreats go, Operation Dynamo, the evacuation of hundreds of thousands of British soldiers from Dunkirk between 27th May and 4th June 1940, has come to be seen as a brilliant success, a heroic nose-thumbing at Hitler, rather than a humiliating defeat of a once mighty imperial power now unmatched against a country that had had little military capability less than a decade before. Amongst other good news stories, contemporary spin focussed on the efforts of leisure boaters taking their own yachts across the Channel, the so-called Little Ships that each brought a handful of Tommies home. It was important for British morale that the public see the fall of France only as a temporary setback in the fight against Hitler, so the version of the Dunkirk evacuation that Winston Churchill's government encouraged saw almost 340,000 Allied troops rescued from France, ensuring that Britain still had an army to repel a German invasion.

But that was only half the story. Surpassing the most pessimistic expectations of the more sober figures in the British government and military, Germany had stormed across western Europe, defeating (and in some parts simply occupying, having met little in the way of organised resistance) Luxembourg, the Netherlands, Belgium and later France in little over a month. The first German units came within sight of the Channel coast at the mouth of the River Somme on 20th May, and, as more followed, they left British, French and Belgian troops trapped in an ever shrinking pocket of northern France. They also ensured that Allied personnel throughout the rest of France had no way of getting to Dunkirk when the evacuation order came on 26th May.

Some 198,000 British troops were evacuated from Dunkirk, but almost as many again were still stranded on the continent. This included a number of armoured and infantry divisions, as well as other units separated from their own divisions. There were also 150,000 operational support personnel, from clerks and cooks to engineers and RAF ground staff. Operation Dynamo ended on 4th June, after the French units providing rear-guard defence surrendered to the German forces advancing on Dunkirk. On 10th June, Operation Cycle began, evacuating over 11,000 more from Le Havre. That ended on 13th June, by which time any British people still left in France were heading to St Nazaire, south of the Brittany salient, having been told ships were awaiting them there. Many of them did not know about what had happened at Dunkirk, in

In some ways the retreat to St Nazaire was even more urgent than the retreat to Dunkirk.

the same way many in Britain did not know so many of their countrymen remained in France.

Operation Ariel constituted the last major British operation on French soil until D-Day almost exactly four years later. Between 14th and 25th June, another 215,000 were evacuated from St Nazaire (and other ports along the west coast), the vast majority of them British, but sizeable numbers of Polish and French troops were also rescued. Included in the number were also plenty of civilians, including diplomatic staff and their children. In some ways the retreat to St Nazaire was even more urgent than the retreat to Dunkirk. Come the end of Operation Ariel, any British people who remained in Europe would probably be there until the end of the war.

St Nazaire was not an ideal location from which to evacuate large numbers of people. Though a major port, it was located in the estuary of the River Loire, and its waters were too shallow for some of the larger vessels that came to St Nazaire. Some had to anchor several miles away and have people brought to them by smaller boats. One of these was the liner RMS *Lancastria*, which could have gone on to be remembered for bringing up to 9,000 evacuees back to Britain. Instead she went on to suffer the worst disaster in British maritime history, which would barely be remembered at all.

From luxury liner to rescue ship

When launched in 1920, Cunard named their new 578ft (176m) liner the *Tyrrhenia*. Built in Clydebank, the Scottish town that grew up around – and was named for – its famous shipyards, the 16,243-ton liner was painted with the same striking black and white livery that the *Titanic* had had. Unlike the *Titanic* she only had one funnel, which was raked slightly towards the stern and painted red. She was one of the first Cunard liners to have a cruiser stern, which reduced water resistance compared to more gently curved sterns. Towering over her sun decks were two masts, one on either side of the funnel.

Across her seven decks she could carry up to 2,200 passengers, initially in three classes but later only two. She was given the name *Tyrrhenia* in the hope that it would appeal to Italians looking to emigrate to America, but in 1921, before the *Tyrrhenia* was even ready for her first voyage, the US government brought in the Immigration Act, which restricted immigration. Her maiden voyage took her from Glasgow to Quebec and Montreal, and later she sailed between Liverpool and New York, but her name proved unpopular with English crew and American passengers. In 1924, having acquired the unflattering nickname Soup Tureen, the *Tyrrhenia* was renamed the *Lancastria*. From 1932 onwards the *Lancastria* spent much of her time cruising the waters of northern Europe and the Mediterranean.

When war broke out between Britain and Germany in September 1939, the *Lancastria* was on a cruise in the Bahamas. She was ordered to New York immediately for a refit, her black and white livery to be painted over in standard battleship grey, and for half a year afterwards she carried cargo. In April 1940 the British government requisitioned the ship from Cunard and used her as a troop transport, carrying soldiers to Norway to defend it from German invasion. A month later, Norway having fallen to the Nazis, the *Lancastria* was back to take those soldiers home again.

Her crew was given shore leave. That wasn't to last long.

Following her return from Norway, the *Lancastria* headed to Liverpool, with the plan that she be dry-docked for an overhaul. Her crew was given shore leave. That wasn't to last long. Only hours later they were all recalled. Under the command of Captain Rudolph Sharp the *Lancastria* was to sail for St Nazaire immediately. Sharp was from a long line of sailors, and had several decades of experience as an officer on cruise liners, having served aboard the *Mauretania*, the *Queen Mary* and the *Titanic*'s sister ship, the *Olympic*. During the First World War he had narrowly escaped another maritime disaster, having left the *Lusitania* just before her final voyage.

'A head in a noose'

By late evening on 16th June, tens of thousands of men around St Nazaire harbour were practising that most British of arts – queuing. This particular queue stretched for five miles. Many of the men had not slept more than a few hours over the previous three days, and some of them had walked all the way from Belgium. One man had dived into a ditch and broken his ankle when a German plane flew overhead, but as the only alternative to keeping on walking was capture by the advancing Wehrmacht, he just tightened his boot and practised that other British art – keeping a stiff upper lip.

Everyone else had raided their stores then set fire to everything they could before leaving for St Nazaire. They grimly accepted the Germans were going to win this one, but at least the promise of going home lifted their spirits. Some French citizens spat at them as they headed to the harbour, but many of the men did not fully understand why – not knowing all the details about what had happened at Dunkirk, they perhaps did not realise that the Allies were in retreat all over Europe and that the fall of France was imminent.

Without the same level of rear-guard defence that French troops had provided for the evacuation from Dunkirk, St Nazaire was being swiftly surrounded. German soldiers were closing in fast, only 25 miles from the harbour as Operation Ariel progressed. But the biggest threat was not from troops approaching over land but from the planes of the Luftwaffe already overhead. German planes had inflicted many of the casualties suffered during the evacuation at Dunkirk, strafing lines of men walking down roads and bombing boats and ships as well as soldiers on the beaches. The men queuing in St Nazaire weren't too bothered by the sound of the planes. By that time they had been listening to the sounds of a sky dominated by the Luftwaffe for weeks, and at least around St Nazaire those sounds were accompanied by a more reassuring one – that of the RAF's Hurricanes on patrol.

The *Lancastria* reached the River Loire estuary overnight and anchored at 4am on the 17th. A misty dawn gave way to bright sunshine and the promise of a warm summer afternoon with calm waters, which was ideal. Captain

Sharp was dismayed that they were still miles from the harbour, knowing that loading men from tenders would cause unpredictable delays. But the bay being so shallow, they had no choice. If the *Lancastria* got any closer she risked running aground, or being unable to turn. Sharp noted what a French skipper told him – that anchoring there was like putting his head in a noose – then carried on with his mission.

Sharp was to 'load as many men as possible without regard to the limits set down under international law'.

At around 6am Royal Navy officers boarded the *Lancastria* and demanded that Sharp take as many men as he could possibly fit on board. A civilian captain on a requisitioned vessel, Sharp knew he was in no position to argue, but he made it perfectly clear in the log what they had told him, that he was to 'load as many men as possible without regard to the limits set down under international law'. Whether that order came from the naval officers on the ground or whether they were simply passing the message down from the Admiralty is not known, for the same reason much of the official version of events is not known, and won't be until 2040.

As the first tenders arrived at about 7am, the *Lancastria*'s crew rehearsed a boat drill. With German bombers trying to reach other vessels in harbour, and reports of U-boat movements in the area too, the *Lancastria*'s officers wanted to be ready for any eventuality. However, their preparations did not anticipate just how many of those waiting in St Nazaire that the ship would be expected to take.

Sharp wanted to limit the number coming aboard to 3,000, which was already well above the legal limit of

2,200. He was ignored by those co-ordinating the evacuation from the harbour. His stewards lost count after about 6,000 had boarded the *Lancastria*, but they kept on coming for several hours more. By the time Sharp decided enough was enough, at 2pm, an unknown number of people crowded his vessel. Lower estimates suggest at least 7,500 were on board. The upper estimate stands in excess of 9,000.

Lambs to the slaughter

Despite the drab military paintjob, the *Lancastria* was still a luxury liner at heart. The military hadn't ripped out all of the lavish accoutrements that her high class (and high paying) passengers expected, so she still had a luxurious dining room designed like a Renaissance parlour, she still had various saloon bars, a gym and a couple of swimming pools. Her crew still included the stewards, who continued to wear their pristine white uniforms with polished gold buttons.

It was an astonishing juxtaposition for many of the soldiers who started coming aboard just after 7am. Many of these working class men would never have been aboard a liner unless they had worked on one in peacetime, but now in wartime they left the bombed towns of France, rode out of harbour in a small overcrowded tender, then had to climb up the rope netting thrown over the towering sides of the *Lancastria*. It was like climbing up the outside of a building, but when they got on deck they were greeted by stewards and invited to the dining room for a silver service breakfast. Waiters brought hot tea and coffee, freshly baked bread, eggs, bacon, sausages, porridge and citrus fruit. For many this was the first hot meal they had had in weeks. After filling up they even had the option of visiting the on-board barbershop for a shave.

The first to board were given little tickets with their cabin number, but as the tenders continued to go back and forth throughout the morning and past lunchtime, the cabins quickly filled and men were directed towards the holds instead. Lifejackets were offered to all to begin with, but some men only took them because they thought the lifejackets would make useful pillows. Those who had not slept properly for days looked for somewhere quiet to lie down and get some immediate rest, and the bowels of the ship seemed the best place for that.

The *Lancastria*'s holds were the size of warehouses. Mattresses lined the floor with hardly room to step between them. Dim electric bulbs set into the walls and covered by thick glass plates provided the only light, but it was at the perfect level

The men only took lifejackets because they thought they would make useful pillows.

for those who wanted to get to sleep straight away. Those suffering seasickness went to the hold at the very bottom of the ship, close to the engine room. It was hot, stuffy and, with so many crowding in, quite airless too, but the truly exhausted didn't care. One man, however, retorted that the dimly lit hold full of unconscious figures reminded him of a morgue, and he decided to head back up on deck. It was a decision he unlikely regretted. Few of those who settled at the bottom of the ship survived.

Whilst the first on board may have got the silver service treatment, by the time the last were allowed aboard just before 2pm, they were lucky if they could make their way through the crowds to reach the dining room for a cup of tea. The *Lancastria* was now so overcrowded that a major was sent to a cabin with four bunks only to find seven other officers already sharing them. When the major complained to the purser, the purser told him three more men would be joining them shortly, and they would be sleeping on the floor. And two of them were colonels.

The last to board couldn't even get inside. They would have to spend the journey squeezed onto the open deck. Most were not too bothered, because it was only a relatively short trip – 300 miles – around Ushant and across the Channel to reach Britain, and they were simply glad to have not been captured by the Germans. Lifejackets had long since run out, but nobody was particularly bothered about that either. High spirits reigned, and as the men were jostled into tighter and tighter spaces an infectious chorus of sheep noises spread amongst them.

The Lancastria *was now so overcrowded that a major was sent to a cabin with four bunks only to find seven other officers already sharing them.*

Attacks from the air

At 1.50pm, German bombers appeared in the sky. Less than a mile away from the *Lancastria* another liner, the 20,000-ton *Oronsay*, also lay at anchor as boats brought men to her from St Nazaire too. There was nothing the crews of either ship could do to evade a bombing but they used their ships' klaxons to signal that an air raid was imminent. This time the *Lancastria* escaped undamaged. A bomb hit the *Oronsay*'s bridge and killed several officers and crewmen, but did no major structural damage.

Shortly thereafter Captain Sharp ordered the rope netting be retracted, the sally ports in the sides of the ship shut, and the small boats milling around the *Lancastria* turned away. The captain of a nearby destroyer, HMS *Havelock*, recommended that Sharp leave for Britain as soon as possible. The Germans were closing in. Those bombers had surely reported the liners' positions, and there were also reports of U-boats in the area. Sharp requested an escort across the Channel, a destroyer like the *Havelock* that might be able to detect submarines and drop depth charges, or at the very least make the *Lancastria* look less vulnerable than she was. But the *Havelock* had to remain at St Nazaire until the operation was complete. So Sharp decided to wait too. More worried about submarines than aircraft, he thought it would be safer to travel with another ship, whether a warship or another liner like the *Oronsay*. His chief officers all concurred.

Some of those below deck may have disagreed. Men near portholes in the lower decks watched the bomber attack on the *Oronsay* and started to make their way up top. If the *Lancastria* fell victim to a major air raid, they realised, it would be just as dangerous to be stuck at the bottom of the ship as it would be to be standing on deck. Those on deck weren't quite so bothered. They had waited the longest to board the ship and now they were enjoying the warm mid-afternoon sun. Those fighting their way up to the top found other unconcerned men sleeping on the stairs or playing cards on the floor in passageways.

Sharp intended to leave at about 4pm, but he had left it too late. At 3.48pm, when the captain was in his cabin, the lookouts spotted more incoming planes and they were not the RAF's patrolling Hurricanes. They were the Luftwaffe's Junker bombers, and this time they were coming straight for the sitting duck *Lancastria*.

The *Lancastria*'s klaxons signalled another air raid, but there was no panic amongst men who had been listening to planes and sirens for weeks. Alarm below decks resulted in nothing more than a few portholes being closed in case a bomb landing in the water sent a surge of water against the hull. As the first Junkers passed overhead and their bombs completely missed the *Lancastria*, those watching from the sun deck laughed and jeered. Their laughter didn't last long. Those manning anti-aircraft guns on the deck of the *Lancastria* tried to drive the Junkers away, but the planes kept coming. Their 500lb bombs got closer and closer.

In quick succession, three direct hits sealed the Lancastria's fate.

In quick succession, three direct hits sealed the *Lancastria*'s fate. Few on board would have doubted these were mortal wounds. Those who saw the explosions were temporarily blinded by flashes like sheet lightning. Everyone else on the ship heard the deafening sound, like they were inside a thunder cloud. The explosions smashed much of the glass on the *Lancastria*. For a few moments the ship was plunged into darkness, but the lights soon flickered back on. The stricken vessel continued to buck and shudder long after the debris had settled.

The bombs had exploded in holds 2, 3 and 4. One of them smashed through the restaurant, where men were eating, and exploded beneath it, tearing a hole in the hull and causing some of the restaurant to cave in on top of the diners.

Some 800 RAF personnel were in hold 2. The bomb detonated as it crashed through the hatch overhead. Turning the metal into shrapnel, the bomb killed nearly everyone in that hold instantly. Many were decapitated. Most of those who survived would live long enough to discover the explosion had destroyed their escape routes, before fire and thick black smoke overcame them.

Many survivors later claimed that one of the bombs went down the *Lancastria*'s funnel. Officers on the bridge corroborated this story because immediately after the attack they tried to contact the engine room but couldn't get a response, so assumed it had been destroyed. However, all of the

It was in the middle of a spreading oil slick that the Lancastria *began to sink.*

crew in the engine room survived, despite it being so deep inside the ship. They escaped through an engineering duct that led all the way up to the main deck. One of the survivors had been standing on the platform above the boiler room during the air raid, and a bomb falling down the funnel would have destroyed that platform and killed him. The bomb actually fell into hold 4, which was immediately behind the bridge. From a certain angle it would appear like it had gone down the funnel instead. This bomb tore a hole in the port side below the waterline. Smoke from the explosion soon enveloped the entire bow of the ship.

The bomb that hit hold 3 ruptured fuel tanks. Fortunately the explosion didn't set fire to the oil, but 1,400 tons spilled out into the water. It was in the middle of a spreading oil slick that the *Lancastria* began to sink.

Twenty minutes to live

Captain Sharp, who had been in his cabin when the air raid began, rushed to the bridge as his ship developed a noticeable list to starboard. If he hadn't feared the worst before he got there, what he saw when he joined his officer of the watch must have left him with no doubts. Looking down through the churning smoke, past the panicking men trying to escape in every direction, he saw the rush of white water bursting up through the middle of the ship from hold 4. The *Lancastria* was going down by the head and listing ever further to starboard. Sharp gave the order to abandon ship.

Those nearest the side of the ship could look overboard and see water flooding into a gaping hole in the hull.

Amidst the chaos of a sinking ship overcrowded to perhaps more than four times capacity, any order would struggle to circulate. Many men didn't need to hear it from the captain anyway. Those nearest the side of the ship could look overboard and see water flooding into a gaping hole in the hull. As soon as the *Lancastria* started to list, the cry went up around those on deck to jump overboard. Soldiers began jumping by the dozen.

Officers struggling to maintain some sense of order and control used megaphones to order crewmen to clear away the lifeboats. Other orders were given to lower ropes into the rapidly flooding forehold, but too many in the hold grabbed the ropes at the same time. It was impossible to pull any of them up, and none of them managed to climb up either.

Suddenly the ship lurched. For a few seconds everyone on board must have assumed the *Lancastria* was entering

BRITAIN'S DARKEST HOUR 107

her death roll. She listed so badly to starboard that men still jumping from her port side risked death by dropping 70ft (20m) to the water. On the starboard side, however, her gunwale was so close to the water that men could simply step off into the sea. Realising that the crowds pouring up on to the top deck had made the *Lancastria* top heavy, and that this rather than her water intake was causing the imminent capsize, the officers with the megaphones ordered as many over to the port side as would listen.

Seemingly miraculously for those still below decks, unaware of what was going on above them, the *Lancastria* slowly levelled off. She had given them a reprieve, extra time to try and escape. But it would not last long. Gradually, as she took on more and more water, the *Lancastria* began rolling to port, and this time moving scared young soldiers around the sun deck would not be enough to save her.

> Steam from fractured pipes hissed into companionways. Men held handkerchiefs to their faces so that they wouldn't get burnt.

A strong smell of explosives seeped through the cabins and companionways as thousands of men struggled to find a way out. They found passages destroyed by the explosions and exits blocked by fire. Men from the Auxiliary Pioneer Corps tried to unravel fire hoses, but the crush of those desperate to escape made it impossible to fight the flames. Steam from fractured pipes hissed into companionways. Men held handkerchiefs to their faces so that they wouldn't get burnt.

In some parts of the ship's bowels those who managed to survive reported a very British, very orderly evacuation.

Out of these reports came the story of Father Charles McMenemy, one of the heroes of the *Lancastria*'s final moments. A Roman Catholic priest, McMenemy had been in France to serve as chaplain for the troops. With nobody else to lead them, no orders and no idea which way to go, men were attracted to the padre's calm, quiet authority. He led a group of men through ankle-deep waters at the bottom of the ship and found a way out in the side of the ship. They were only 6ft (1.8m) above the waterline. McMenemy recommended the soldiers ditch as much of their heavy uniforms as possible before they jumped in, because the clothes would only weigh the men down and make it harder for them to swim. When a sergeant-major without a lifejacket revealed he couldn't swim, McMenemy gave the officer his own lifejacket. Then he jumped in too.

This was far divorced from the chaos happening elsewhere. Men kicked through locked wooden doors looking for a way out. A young soldier, nerves already shredded by weeks on the run from the Germans, became hysterical. Others quickly shoved him into a cabin to calm him down and to stop the hysteria spreading. In one episode, bordering on slapstick, a slim man managed to slip through a porthole and then a somewhat less slim man tried to copy him. He promptly got stuck and called for a push. That only wedged him in tighter. Eventually they gave up and pulled him back inside instead.

A young soldier, nerves already shredded by weeks on the run from the Germans, became hysterical.

But panic really took hold when water started trickling down the stairs. The water had actually pooled inside the ship when the *Lancastria* listed to starboard and was now simply flowing through the ship, gravity carrying it to the lowest point, as she listed to port. But to the men stuck below, this was a sign that the ship was about to go under.

A fight broke out on the main staircase. Men still carrying their rifles, still wearing their heavy packs as ordered by their ranking officers, surged forward into a bottleneck on every deck. Those at the very bottom of the ship, still waiting to get a foot on the first step, were already treading water, which was rising rapidly.

The wooden staircase could not bear the weight of so many men. When it collapsed it ensured that several thousand men would have no chance of survival.

The wooden staircase could not bear the weight of so many men. When it collapsed it ensured that several thousand men would have no chance of survival. They didn't have enough time to find another way out. Though they would have spent the rest of their lives looking, that was soon rendered impossible. The lights went out, and this time they did not flicker back on again. For those nearing the top of the stairs there was the faint promise of daylight above. Everyone else was now trapped in darkness.

Time running out

The *Lancastria* carried 32 lifeboats, each capable of taking about 100 people, which left two thirds of those aboard without a place. Ultimately it was inconsequential that the *Lancastria* did not have enough boats for everyone. In the 20 minutes she took to sink only two were launched successfully. The crew ordered to launch them found many of the davits rusted. Soldiers struck the davits with the butts of their rifles to try and clear them, but it was soon too late. The *Lancastria* quickly listed at such an angle that no more lifeboats could be launched.

In addition to the two boats that got away, another two lifeboats were filled and began to be lowered. One of them became stuck when it was still hanging from the ropes only halfway down. This boat carried women, children and other civilians. A man lost several fingers trying to force a rope through the pulley. Another, a member of the Pioneer Corps manning the lifeboat, took out his knife and cut the rope. Not realising his error until it was too late, he was thrown into the sea along with everyone else in the boat as it fell and then dangled from the one remaining rope at the other end. Another lifeboat also capsized before it reached the water.

As those on deck began to realise they were not going to escape the ship in a lifeboat, many began to leap.

As those on deck began to realise they were not going to escape the ship in a lifeboat, many who had ignored the earlier suggestion to jump began to leap. One soldier, still more reticent than his comrades, looked over the side to see again how far it was from the top deck to the water's surface. In doing so he saved his life. He saw what looked like coconuts floating below him and realised they were decapitated human heads. Other motionless soldiers floated nearby too. By jumping over the side whilst wearing a lifejacket, these men had broken their necks. The force of hitting the water made the lifejacket snap up. The reticent soldier removed his lifejacket, threw it over the side, then jumped in after it. He survived.

Meanwhile others without lifejackets hurried back into the cabins and lounges, looking for anything that would float when they threw it overboard. Most of these makeshift floats landed on somebody already in the water. The sheer number of people in the sea made it just as hard for those in the water to swim away as it was for those wanting to jump in to do so without hitting anyone. Some men started to climb down rope ladders instead, stepping on fingers and heads in their haste. Others slid down ropes cast over the side, searing the skin off their palms as they descended too quickly.

As the *Lancastria* went down by the head, men found it harder not to lose their footing. Some stumbled and then tumbled down the listing deck. The ever increasing pitch also made it difficult for those trying to jump from the rising stern, not least because that was now like jumping from the roof of a tall building. The men took running jumps over the railing. Many misjudged the distance and slid down the hull, getting stranded on the rusted propeller shaft housing, now 30ft (9m) above the sea.

Those still coming up from below decks reached the bright, blinding sunlight and found that the lack of lifeboats – or even reasonable alternatives to lifeboats – was not actually the most pressing threat. German planes continued to take *One man manned his anti-aircraft gun until the water swept him away.* runs at the *Lancastria*, but instead of dropping more bombs they strafed the men. Bullet holes pocked the decks. Men who had tried to drive the bombers away with anti-aircraft fire continued to fire back at the planes, even as the bow disappeared beneath the surface and the waterline rushed up the deck. Elsewhere men were still trying to release rafts and lifeboats until the water washed over them and swelled the ropes, making untying knots impossible. One man manned his anti-aircraft gun until the water swept him away.

The *Lancastria's* death roll

At 4.08pm, only 20 minutes after the attack, the *Lancastria* slowly rolled over to port. Her sirens, which had wailed the entire time, were finally silenced. The men who had not jumped beforehand, including many of those who were unable to swim, simply floated off the deck as she capsized. The *Lancastria* settled rapidly, but hundreds of men clambered on top of the upturned hull. Some found dry cigarettes and decided they were unlikely to stay that way for long, so smoked them whilst they could. They knew there was nothing they could do to help those they had seen trapped inside the ship on the other side of portholes. As German planes returned once again to strafe the hull, many of those standing on it linked arms and began to sing British standards, starting with *Roll Out the Barrel*, then *Hanging Out the Washing on the Siegfried Line* and, as the ship sank, *There'll Always Be an England*.

There was a gentle swell as the *Lancastria* disappeared beneath the sea, but the downdraught sucked hundreds underwater. Many of those who couldn't swim only floated back to the surface after they drowned. A later investigation suggested that whilst the *Lancastria* could never have survived the damage she suffered, she should have stayed afloat for much longer. Her watertight bulkheads should have stopped her flooding so rapidly. Perhaps the number of people crowded into the belly of the ship, below the waterline, ensured the bulkheads would never have been sealed in time, not without sentencing thousands to death. Most died anyway, but by keeping the bulkheads open everyone was at least given the chance to try and escape.

Several thousand people now floated in the spot where the *Lancastria* sank, amidst a field of debris that included smashed wood, deckchairs, clothes, kitbags and lifejackets. The fight for those began immediately. Elsewhere men realised only cooperation would save lives – they formed groups of six, gathered in circles, three of them with lifejackets ensuring the men without lifejackets between them stayed afloat. Other flotsam became essential flotation devices for those who couldn't swim, as well as those who would have to wait until early evening before rescue. Some of those who couldn't swim desperately grabbed at those who could. Swimmers surrounded by non-swimmers realised they had to dive beneath the grasping arms to escape. People began to drown.

For the German planes still circling overhead, the black-coated sea and the tell-tale rainbow swirls of leaked oil proved an irresistible target.

Many found themselves splashing in oil. Some 1,400 tons had leaked out of hold 3, and the slick continued to spread around the survivors. Oil blinded plenty, and choked those who accidentally swallowed it, drowning many. And for the German planes still circling overhead, the black-coated sea and the tell-tale rainbow swirls of leaked oil proved an irresistible target. Men in the water realised the planes were dropping incendiaries, and firing at the water not just to shoot survivors, but to set the oil on fire. Men were lifted out of the water as the bombs exploded beneath the surface. The concussion created by each detonation felt like a thump in the belly. The blasts generated waves that swept men a long way, and filled the air with a heavy spray of oil.

But the Germans failed to ignite the oil slick. Flames flickered across small patches of oil, but the slick had now dispersed so widely that the flames did not spread. The pilots turned their attentions to the lifeboats instead, even though they mainly carried women and children. Flying low, the planes shot one of the boats to pieces.

It would take hours to reach those in the middle of the crowd, in which time many would drown.

Watching the spurts of bullets hitting the water as the Germans indiscriminately targeted survivors, a man on a raft took out his pistol and shot himself.

By the time the *Lancastria* sank, word had already reached St Nazaire of the impending catastrophe and vessels of all sizes were rushing out to rescue as many as they could. When they arrived on the chaotic scene, the task seemed almost insurmountable. So many were struggling in the water that it would take hours to reach those in the middle of the crowd, in which time many would drown. Some officers had ordered their men not to abandon their rifles and kitbags, and they drowned under the weight. As desperate men swam for the remaining lifeboat, an officer on board it shot at them to prevent the boat being swamped. But other men in the water kept up their spirits by continuing to sing rousing songs as they awaited rescue. Many shed their clothes and boots to make it easier to swim and stay afloat, and when they eventually boarded the rescue vessels they did so naked or wearing only underwear. Like everyone else, however, they had to swim through the dead to reach the boats offering life.

The other ships involved in Operation Ariel were already overladen with evacuees too, even if most of them weren't as big as the *Lancastria*. There wasn't much room for any more, but they all took as many as they could. Launches from the P&O liners *Strathaird* and *Strathnaver* brought survivors aboard, and the destroyer HMS *Highlander* found room for more too. Merchant vessels, including the cargo ship SS *John Holt* and the trawler *Cambridgeshire*, took over 1,000 between them. Even a minesweeper that could take no more aboard towed an overfilled lifeboat behind her.

Out of the water came stories of heroism and miraculous survival, not just unimaginable horror. Jacqueline Tillyer was the youngest survivor. Only two years old, she had been in the restaurant with her parents when the bombs hit. Even though they were anxious to get off themselves, the soldiers all forced the family through the crowd ahead of them, and then insisted Jacqueline's father join his wife and child in the lifeboat. This chivalry saved both father and daughter, because the lifeboat was one of the ones that sank. It was *And amongst all the human survivors there were also a couple of dogs too, including a mongrel that belonged to two Belgian children.* three hours before the Tillyer family were picked up by the *Highlander*, and during that time Jacqueline's father held onto her by gripping her clothes in his teeth.

Father McMenemy, who had already saved the lives of those he led to safety through the bottom of the flooding ship, swam for 45 minutes before being picked up by a French tug. He then spent the rest of the day hauling others out of the water. He wasn't the only survivor to immediately join the rescue efforts. A man covered in oil dived into the sea again and again to drag flailing non-swimmers to the side of a rescue boat where they could be pulled out. Amongst all of the human survivors there were a couple of dogs too, including a mongrel that belonged to two Belgian children. Neither of the children survived.

Given what had happened to the *Lancastria*, and without food, an escort and in some cases any radio capability, it might have been safer for the vessels around St Nazaire to return to France and surrender to the approaching Germans rather than attempt to make it back to Britain. None of them did. Even injured men taken back to shore by a French fishing boat later chose a risky night-time crossing (standing up the whole way) on a collier rather than remain in France under Red Cross protection. The captain of the *Oronsay* had broken his leg when the planes destroyed his bridge but he too chose to limp back to Britain using the auxiliary steering gear, a handheld sextant and his own memory. His ship had taken on 3ft (1m) of water after being holed, but the pumps kept her water intake at bay long enough to reach home. The pumps failed less than half an hour later.

About 23,000 were evacuated from St Nazaire that day, including 2,477 survivors from the *Lancastria*. That number also included many who were seriously wounded, such as those who had swallowed oil, and who died later. As the survivors headed back to Britain they heard the news – France had surrendered to Germany, and the previous day Philippe Petain had signed the Vichy agreement with the Nazis. Soon the survivors would share in the gloom of their countrymen, but for at least one day they could simply be glad to be alive.

Officially forgotten

The first five weeks of his premiership came to define Winston Churchill's career and secure his legend. Three of the four speeches for which he is most famous were made in just over a month. In his first speech as Prime Minister on 13th May he claimed to offer only 'blood, toil, tears and sweat'. Three weeks later, as Germany overran most of Europe, he pledged to 'fight on the beaches'. And on 18th June, the day after the sinking of the *Lancastria*, he not only coined the phrase 'Battle of Britain', but prophesised that a thousand years later people would still call it Britain's 'finest hour'. Had Germany won the war, these speeches, coming in such quick succession, would seem like increasingly desperate rhetoric. But Churchill understood that nothing would ensure a German victory more than a British belief in its inevitability. That is why the evacuation of Dunkirk was recast as a tactical move and a great success, and why the government suppressed any reporting of the *Lancastria*'s fate.

Because the Ministry of Defence's records on the disaster were sealed for 100 years, there is no official death toll, just a range of estimates. The British government accepted that over 1,700 died – those people whose presence on the ship could be confirmed but who were not amongst the survivors. But seeing as the *Lancastria*'s crew lost count of the numbers boarding after about 6,000, and only 2,477 survived, the lowest possible number of fatalities would still be over 3,000. The memorial to the disaster by the beach at St Nazaire commemorates more than 4,000 deaths, but it's likely that even this figure could underestimate the true scale of the loss by several thousand.

If the higher figure is accurate then it accounts for one third of all the men the British Army lost between the declaration of war in September 1939 and the fall of France the following June. Many of those who died on the *Lancastria* were listed as missing in action, as if they had been lost on the battlefield, even when survivors knew they had been on the ship with them.

Churchill ordered the issue of a D-Notice, an official request to the media not to cover stories that might have an effect on national security. Contrary to popular misconception a D-Notice was not legally enforceable, but for five weeks every newspaper in Britain

Many of those who died on the Lancastria were listed as missing in action, as if they had been lost on the battlefield.

complied. The fall of France was a far bigger story anyway. *The New York Times* broke the story in the United States, and on 26th July *The Scotsman* finally broke the British media's silence. The chance of a scoop gone, other newspapers followed suit. *The Daily Herald* made it front page news and the *Sunday Express* printed a photo taken from the *Highlander* of men on the *Lancastria*'s capsized hull. But the story did not run for long, not least because the Battle of Britain was just beginning, but also because many survivors – and indeed rescuers too – refused to talk about what had happened for fear of court martial. For years after the war, everything that was known about Britain's worst maritime disaster was pieced together from what little was said by those who dared to say anything at all, such as crewmen revealing just how many they let on board.

To this day the British government refuses to designate the wreck of the *Lancastria* a war grave, and as late as

2007 a freedom of information request for Ministry of Defence documents regarding the disaster was rejected. In 2040 the official report will cease to be protected by the Official Secrets Act. Some survivors, campaigners on their behalf, and many historians suspect that the reason it was sealed for 100 years is because it will confirm that the order Captain Sharp received to ignore the legal limits and take thousands extra came direct from the Admiralty. Compensation claims against the government would depend on who gave Sharp the order, and by 2040 everyone who survived the *Lancastria* will be dead.

The *Lancastria* Survivors Association was set up after the war to ensure the disaster was not forgotten, campaigning for greater recognition by the British government and supporting survivors. It dissolved in 2010, but its work is continued by the *Lancastria* Association of Scotland. The *Lancastria* was a Scottish-built ship and many of her crew were Scottish, but the *Lancastria* Association of Scotland has become international in scope, with the mayor of St Nazaire its honorary president. Petitioning the Scottish Parliament to recognise the endurance of the survivors and the sacrifice of those who died, the association had great success in 2008 when First Minister Alex Salmond awarded the first commemorative medal to survivors. The medal is available to all survivors (whether Scottish or not), and the immediate next of kin of both survivors and victims. The work of the association to secure the same level of recognition from the British government continues.

6

THE AGE OF TOTAL LOSS

Tragedy without triumph during the Second World War

For one survivor of the sinking of the *Lancastria*, it was the second lucky escape of his long career at sea. Captain Sharp left the *Lusitania* before she sailed on her final voyage but he stayed on the bridge of the *Lancastria* until she sank. He then spent four hours in the water, covered in oil, until pulled into a lifeboat. Though no charges were brought against Sharp, and officially his record went untarnished, he had a good idea how many people lost their lives on his vessel, and the disaster weighed heavily upon him. He was also in command of the 19,695-ton Cunard liner RMS *Laconia* in September 1942 when she was torpedoed in the Atlantic off western Africa. There would be no third lucky escape. Aware that most of the more than 3,000 aboard the *Laconia* would die, Sharp was last seen going into his cabin and locking the door behind himself.

Before being requisitioned by the Admiralty in 1939 and converted to a troop transport in 1941, the *Laconia* had cruised the world, taking up to 2,200 passengers between 22 ports around the globe. On her final voyage she carried hundreds of British and Polish soldiers, 80 civilians, and 1,800 Italian prisoners of war captured in North Africa. As the Axis powers controlled the Mediterranean, Sharp's route back to Britain went the long way, around the Cape of Good Hope. She was by 1942 an old ship, having been at sea for 20 years, and was in need of maintenance. Her barnacle-encrusted hull slowed her down from 16 knots, and her tired engines produced lots of smoke from her funnel, which made her easy to spot. Following her

The only disaster for which survivors said they would happily shake the hand of the man who caused it.

requisition a couple of years before she had been fitted with eight 6-inch guns and two 3-inch guns, sufficient armaments to make her a legitimate military target. Blacked out, she looked like a military target too. Just after 8pm on the 12th, U-boat U-156 patrolling between Liberia and the Ascension Islands spotted her silhouette, and closed to 2 miles (3.2km).

What happened next became known as the *Laconia* Incident. With 1,649 fatalities, the loss of the ship was far from the deadliest sinking of the Second World War, but it is perhaps the only one for which survivors said they would happily shake the hand of the man who caused it.

Two torpedoes hit the *Laconia*, and the old ship's hull buckled, rivets bursting out of their seams at such speed they killed people as if they were bullets. The *Laconia* stopped dead in the water immediately and began listing to starboard, settling heavily by the stern. Below decks some Polish soldiers refused to unlock the pens holding the Italian prisoners. Elsewhere soldiers took mercy on the enemy, resulting in hundreds of Italian soldiers storming through the ship in a running battle with British soldiers who were armed, but who were outnumbered considerably. The *Laconia* had had enough lifeboats for everyone on board, including the prisoners, but some of the 32 boats had been destroyed in the attack, and others could not be launched as the *Laconia* rose further and further towards the vertical. Of more than 20 that got away, most were half empty whilst others sank through overcrowding.

When the U-boat crew heard the *Laconia*'s distress call they realised she was not the troop transport they had assumed she was. The U-boat surfaced, broadcasting its own position in English and requesting assistance from any ships in the area. Drifting in the middle of the Atlantic, even the survivors who made it into the lifeboats had little chance of being rescued. The *Laconia* sank just after 9pm, by which point hundreds had been pulled from the water. The German submariners took as many below as the U-boat could fit, then allowed the rest to huddle on deck. The Germans gave them dry clothes, hot tea and bread. Towing four lifeboats behind, U-156 continued on the surface to rendezvous with several Vichy French ships. They did not get far before an American B-24 Liberator plane spotted this inexplicable convoy. Though the

Germans signalled for assistance, and had stretched a white sheet painted with the sign of the Red Cross across the deck, American planes from the Ascension Islands were ordered to attack. One bomb hit one of the lifeboats under tow.

The U-boat captain had no choice but to abandon the survivors of the *Laconia*. He gave them fresh water, then ordered those on deck back into the sea, and cast the lifeboats adrift. Then U-156 dived slowly, so as not to drag those in the water down. Over half of those who had survived the sinking of the *Laconia* died before the Vichy French ships picked them up. After the incident, Kriegsmarine commander-in-chief Admiral Doenitz issued the *Laconia* Order, which forbade U-boat captains from doing anything to help survivors of their attacks. This paved the way for unrestricted submarine warfare, a policy that Germany's enemies also adopted. The actions of U-156's captain could have set the sinking of the *Laconia* apart from the other maritime tragedies of the Second World War. Instead they inspired a diktat that ensured there would be many more.

Hellships of the Pacific

Between 1942 and 1945, the Japanese transported over 125,000 Allied prisoners of war and Indonesian slave labourers around the Pacific on vessels that became known as 'hellships'. These hellships were usually old, slow, medium-sized freighters unsuited to the task of carrying thousands of men. The only concession the Japanese made towards converting them was to build bamboo scaffolding in the holds, adding a split level so that another layer of men could be packed in on top of those below. A ship like the *Junyo Maru* – a 5,065-ton merchantman, only 405ft (123m) long – had to carry upwards of 5,000 prisoners. Packed into the holds, the low bamboo ceiling prevented them from standing up, and the number of people in there with them prevented them from lying down too. Men spent entire journeys kneeling or squatting because there wasn't even room to sit. Sometimes those journeys lasted for weeks.

Predictably, conditions in the holds quickly became appalling. Even in cooler months the heat inside the almost airless holds was oppressive. In summer it became lethal. The floor of one of the holds on the *Junyo Maru* was sticky with black resin. On a previous trip the freighter had carried a cargo of sugar that had melted and congealed in the heat. The Japanese guards only let a small number of prisoners up on deck to use the toilets – wooden boxes hanging over the side of the ship – at a time, and queuing to go up took hours. The sick, the injured and those weakened by a diet of thin tea, watery stew, rice and boiled vegetables couldn't make it up on deck. Unsanitary conditions prevailed, and the smell was almost unbearable. Many men had boarded with malaria, but dysentery also became rife. In the permanent semi-darkness of holds lit only by faint blue-painted bulbs, it was sometimes hours before anyone noticed yet another death.

Even in cooler months the heat inside the almost airless holds was oppressive. In summer it became lethal.

The prisoners occupied themselves by sharing whatever books they had brought with them or playing card games. Some kept their spirits up by devising daring fantasy plans to take over the ships, using their numerical advantage to overwhelm their Japanese captors. Some hoped to sail into a storm that would cause the ship to founder so that they could either escape or die. Some imagined joining the queue to go up on deck and then letting themselves fall into the sea. Others wished one of their own submarines would spot the unmarked hellship and sink it. On 18th September 1944, that is what happened to the *Junyo Maru*.

By late summer 1944 it became clear that General Douglas MacArthur's forces would retake the Philippines. The Japanese began moving large numbers of prisoners away from the invading forces and to parts of Indonesia where they could shore up Japanese defences. The *Junyo Maru* set sail for Padang on the west coast of Sumatra with about 2,000 Dutch, British, Australian and American prisoners of war. They were joined by 4,200 Javanese slaves. Hellships often took such large labour forces to work on major projects, such as repairing bombed airstrips. The *Junyo Maru*'s human cargo was intended to work on a new railway line across Sumatra that would improve Japan's coal supply line.

The hellship took only 15 minutes to sink against the sunset; time in which thousands of panicking prisoners trapped in the lethally overcrowded, swiftly flooding holds fought to climb up the only ladder to the top deck.

British submarine HMS *Tradewind* had a defective periscope and her radar wasn't working properly either, but neither would have made much difference to the *Junyo Maru*'s fate. The Geneva Convention required ships to bear the Red Cross when they were carrying prisoners but hellships never did. The *Tradewind* fired four torpedoes and hit the *Junyo Maru* with two of them. The hellship took only 15 minutes to sink against the sunset; time in which most of the Japanese escaped, but thousands of panicking prisoners trapped in the lethally overcrowded, swiftly flooding holds fought to climb up the only ladder to the top deck.

Of the more than 5,000 prisoners on board, only about 700 survived a night in the water to be picked up by a Japanese corvette and gunboat the next day. Hardly any of the Javanese survived. Most of them being unable to swim, they huddled at the bow until the *Junyo Maru* sank beneath them. Any relief the others felt at surviving the disaster would have been short lived. All of them went on to work on the railway as planned, working naked but for a loincloth 12 hours a day, 7 days a week for another 11 months in temperatures reaching 50°C (120°F). Fewer than 100 survived the war.

Over 21,000 men died on hellships between 1942 and 1945, and simply because of the number of prisoners crammed aboard, when the ships were targeted and sunk, their losses instantly became some of the deadliest maritime disasters in history, from the 1,540 who died aboard the *Koshu Maru* up to the 3,500 killed when American submarine USS *Rasher* sank the *Tango Maru*. Of all the prisoners of war who died in the Pacific during the Second World War, a third of them were killed by friendly fire at sea. For the US military, the worst single incident was the 24th October 1944 sinking of the *Arisan Maru*, on which 1,776 American prisoners were killed by USS *Shark*.

Most of those aboard the *Arisan Maru* had survived the Bataan Death March in 1942. Following the worst defeat in American military history, almost 80,000 American and Filipino prisoners were marched nearly 100 miles (160km) through the jungle with only one meal in seven days, resulting in the deaths of thousands. Life in the now notorious camps awaiting them at the end of the march was no better, and men often volunteered for work details, not knowing about the hellships that would take them. The *Arisan Maru* left Manila in the Philippines for mainland Japan on 10th October 1944. She was one of the most densely packed of all the hellships. Men had to take it in shifts to sit down in the holds, which had three levels of bamboo shelves with only 3ft (1m) between them. Sailing through a typhoon, most of the prisoners became seasick. With rationed food only served on a first come first served basis, and cruel Japanese guards lowering buckets of urine rather than water, men licked the condensation from the hull to survive as the holds suffered temperatures in excess of 38°C (100°F), even at night.

Their two-week ordeal ended when the *Arisan Maru* was spotted by the crew of the *Shark*, unaware that the unmarked freighter carried so many of their countrymen. The first torpedoes missed. Japanese soldiers and a couple of dozen prisoners who were on deck

Instead of abandoning ship many of the half-starved men stormed the galley, eating as much rice as they could find.

preparing a meal for the others saw the torpedo wakes pass in front of the ship. Three more followed, and they broke the back of the ship. As she buckled in the middle, the stern began to sink, but the bow – where most of the prisoners were – remained relatively level. The Japanese guards cut the rope ladders and locked the hatches on the holds to preventing the prisoners escaping. Then they abandoned ship. The prisoners who had been on deck preparing the meal reopened the hatches and lowered ropes into the hold, but even after coming on deck nobody was in much of a hurry to jump overboard. The forward part of the ship seemed to be sinking so slowly that many hoped the Japanese would come back and repair the vessel. So instead of abandoning ship many of the half-starved men stormed the galley, eating as much rice as they could find. They also filled canteens with water before finally leaving the ship.

They were right to stay on board as long as possible. Even before the *Arisan Maru* sank, two hours after the attack, men had tried swimming over to other vessels in the convoy. The Japanese beat them back. As darkness fell, nearly two thousand men found themselves abandoned in increasingly rough waters, watching their last hope sail away into the night. Knowing that no American ships penetrated this deeply into Japanese waters, most simply gave up. Almost miraculously, however, nine men managed to survive. Four drifted through the night and were later picked up by other Japanese vessels. Five others climbed into an abandoned lifeboat and sailed for the Chinese coast, near which they encountered a Chinese junk. The men went on to be smuggled across China to a US airbase and were repatriated in time for Christmas. Back in America they told their stories from the beginning to a shocked American public that had thus far been largely oblivious to the cruelty of the Pacific war. Learning of the many atrocities, America could no longer be under any illusion as to whom she was fighting.

Unfriendly fire

During the Second World War there was only one vessel ship sunk by US forces that the American government acknowledged they should never have sunk: the 11,249-ton *Awa Maru*. The 502ft (153m) liner had been used as a prisoner transport during 1944 but in 1945 it became a relief ship under the Red Cross banner. As the war turned against Japan, the Allies became increasingly concerned about the prisoners of war in Japanese custody. Through Swiss diplomats (Switzerland having remained as neutral as ever throughout the war), the US government came to an agreement with the Japanese – that they would not attack any ships carrying aid packages to Allied prisoners provided the Japanese informed them of the ships' routes in advance and used floodlights to identify the vessels on passage. The Japanese accepted the agreement not out of humanitarian concerns but because they saw how they could use it to their advantage. When the *Awa Maru* left Singapore on 28th March she not only carried supplies destined for the prison camps, but also 500 tons of munitions and enough crated parts to build 20 aircraft. Some of the 2,004 Japanese passengers on board were military experts too.

The Queenfish *fired four torpedoes into the* Awa Maru, *which then sank in little over two minutes.*

Carrying some aid for imprisoned Americans was meant to guarantee the safety of what would otherwise be a legitimate target. But on the night of 1st April the captain of the *Awa Maru* deviated from the route the Japanese authorities had given the Americans. In the foggy Taiwan Strait the *Awa Maru* was 11 miles off course and 18 miles ahead of schedule. With near zero visibility the overloaded ship, sitting low in the water, looked like a destroyer to the radar operator on submarine USS *Queenfish*. The *Queenfish* fired four torpedoes into the *Awa Maru*, which then sank in little over two minutes. There was only one survivor, steward Kantora Shimoda, who had already survived three sinkings, and when picked up by the *Queenfish* he informed the Americans of their mistake. The *Queenfish* was ordered into Guam, where her commander was stripped of his command and court martialled. The US government feared what would happen to their prisoners if the Japanese abandoned the agreement. As well as acknowledging responsibility for the wrongful sinking, the US even offered the Japanese a replacement ship, but the matter of reparations was dropped following Japan's defeat.

Another ship that the US government should perhaps have acknowledged their forces should not have sunk was the 446ft (136m) *Tsushima Maru*, but being unlit and unmarked the 6,754-ton cargo ship was still a legitimate target. In August 1944 the Pacific war was about to reach the Ryukyu Islands, the most southwesterly point of Japan. The Japanese government knew that the battle for Okinawa would be as pitched as that for Iwo Jima a few months previously, but the difference was that Okinawa had a sizeable population. The Japanese government wanted to evacuate as many children to mainland Japan as possible, but the families had to volunteer to let them go. Teachers were sent to visit them in their homes to convince the parents. The children themselves were gently encouraged to use peer pressure, convincing their friends to go because they were going.

On the morning of 21st August, 767 children were amongst the 1,661 passengers who gathered at the docks. The *Tsushima Maru* was too big to come right up to the dock so anchored offshore, and half a dozen small fishing boats ferried the evacuees to the ship. She seemed to tower over them like a four-storey building, but they still had to climb up rope ladders to reach the deck. The *Tsushima Maru* had been built in Scotland over thirty years before as a cargo ship, and not unlike the hellships, her humid cargo hold was divided into cabins and filled with shelf-like bunks. The crew didn't fill the hold to quite the same density as they did on hellships, of course, and so many children came aboard that some had to stay up on deck. As the ship departed, the children ate the lunches they had brought with them, then took part in an emergency drill, seeing where the white liferafts were located and learning how to use their lifejackets. In the event of needing to abandon ship, they were told, boys should use the ladders to escape the hold, whilst girls should use the stairs.

So many children came aboard that some had to stay up on deck.

The *Tsushima Maru* skirted the edge of a typhoon at about 10pm on her second night at sea, but most of the children slept through it. The submarine USS *Bowfin* was on her sixth patrol mission since being commissioned the year before. Shortly before 10.30pm her crew spotted the *Tsushima Maru*. The dull thud of the *Bowfin*'s torpedoes hitting the ship woke most of the children, who awoke the rest as they clambered over them in a panic. The ship was on fire and the lights had gone out, and those on deck could hear the water rushing in below. As the foundering ship shuddered and groaned, the teachers who had accompanied the evacuees ordered everyone to get ready to jump over the port side. Some started leaping over the deck railing in groups before they were ordered to, but many were still on board, too terrified to jump, as the *Tsushima Maru* went under.

As the children in the water quickly discovered, there was not enough room in the rafts for all of them. With the typhoon descending on their location, the strong currents carried those not on a raft away into the night. The rest had to listen to desperate cries for help coming out of the darkness. Many of them still expected rescue, and sang songs to keep their spirits up, but six days later some were still drifting. Without water, some drank their own urine. Rough seas dispersed the hundreds of survivors, and their numbers dwindled before help arrived.

Some started leaping over the deck railing in groups before they were ordered to, but many were still on board, too terrified to jump.

Only 59 children survived the disaster. Their families heard rumours, but the truth was officially suppressed until after the end of the war. It was decades later before the crew of the *Bowfin* learnt of what they had done. Despite the tragedy that befell the *Tsushima Maru*, those who she left behind in Okinawa didn't fare much better. The battle for the island was just as bad as the Japanese government had feared. Up to a third of the civilian population lost their lives.

Britain's fatal mistakes

The circumstances that led to so many friendly fire deaths in the Pacific were mirrored in Europe, though it was mostly

British rather than American vessels that were responsible. In September 1943, Italy signed an armistice with the Allies. This had been foreseen for months, not least by the Germans, who observed the Allied invasion of Sicily in July and the Italian king's subsequent removal from power of Benito Mussolini, and realised a disarmed Italy would be less threat to the southern flank of the Reich than an Italy that switched sides. Even before the Allies met Italian diplomats in Portugal, Germany sent several divisions across the Alps, telling the Italian government they were coming to shore up Italian defences, but in reality being the spearhead of a German invasion.

Thousands were packed onto unsuitable, unseaworthy, unmarked ships.

Whilst Italian soldiers who had retreated to the mainland to defend against imminent Allied invasion could rely on British support and protection, those in southern France, the occupied Balkans and on Greek islands in the Aegean were quickly overwhelmed. On Rhodes there was a garrison of 40,000 Italian troops, and on Crete another 22,000. The victorious Germans gave the defeated Italians a choice: they could either continue to fight alongside the Germans, or be sent to Germany. Loyal fascists and those afraid of mistreatment chose the former. The vast majority chose the latter. But Hitler considered them traitors, not prisoners of war, and most of them were destined not for prisoner of war camps, but slave labour. Thousands were packed onto unsuitable, unseaworthy, unmarked ships for transport to mainland Greece. These ships were the Nazis' hellships, and they became just as viable targets for unwitting British vessels as Japan's hellships were for American submarines in the Pacific.

The 3,428-ton merchant ship *Gaetano Donizetti* only had room for 700 men in her hold, but at Rhodes the Germans forced between 1,600 and 1,900 Italian sailors and airmen into the bowels of the 15-year-old ship. She set sail from Rhodes on 22nd September with over 200 crew and guards aboard, but the next day the Royal Navy destroyer HMS *Eclipse* spotted her. The *Gaetano Donizetti* had no armour to protect her from the *Eclipse*'s volley and capsized almost immediately, sinking within seconds. There were no survivors.

Souda Bay in northwest Crete became the scene of several disasters. In late October the Germans forced almost 2,700 mainly Italian (though also some Greek) prisoners into the cargo hold of the confiscated French cargo ship *Sinfra*. The 4,470-ton vessel was attacked by American B-25s and the RAF's Beaufighters. The distress signal she sent called for rescue boats, but ordered them to save the 200 German soldiers aboard first. Just over 560 survived, 163 of them German. In February 1944 the British submarine HMS *Sportsman* sighted the German merchant ship *Petrella* just north of Souda Bay and torpedoed her, unaware that she carried a human cargo of 3,173 Italian prisoners. The *Petrella* did not sink immediately, but the German guards refused to open the doors and let the Italians escape. They fired on those who tried. Only 500 of the prisoners survived.

The Petrella *did not sink immediately, but the German guards refused to open the doors and let the Italians escape.*

A British submarine may also have been responsible for the loss of the Norwegian steamer *Oria*. The 2,127-ton ship left Rhodes on 11th February 1944, heading for

Piraeus on the Greek mainland. She was carrying 4,046 Italians, most of them soldiers, as well as over 100 German guards or crewmen. On the second night of the journey she sailed through a storm and ran aground on a reef off Cape Sounion. An uncorroborated theory suggests her crew had spotted a submarine and were trying to evade it when they hit the rocks. The *Oria* quickly broke up, her forepart sinking rapidly whilst her afterpart capsized. In the bad weather even those who could make it out of the ship before she went down drowned. Tugs reached the area the following morning and found only a few dozen survivors, most of them Italians. Nearly 4,100 died, making it the Mediterranean's worst maritime disaster.

Russian prisoners also suffered as a result of British friendly fire, most notably with the sinking of the 3,828-ton Norwegian ship *Rigel*, which had been requisitioned by the occupying German forces in 1940 to transport prisoners of war, German deserters and Norwegian resistance fighters to Germany. In November 1944, the aircraft carrier HMS *Implacable* was involved in Operation Provident, attacking German convoys off the coast of Norway. On the 27th her crew spotted the *Rigel*, which they *Sinking fast, there wasn't time to launch many lifeboats. Panic broke out as the fire spread.* thought was a troop transport because she was being escorted by two naval vessels. Instead she carried thousands of prisoners of war (some sources claim up to 4,500), most of them Russian but also a few hundred Polish and Serbian soldiers. Fairey Barracuda bombers from the *Implacable* landed five direct hits against the *Rigel*, at least one of which hit a storage compartment holding prisoners, and the rest of which set the ship ablaze. Sinking fast, there wasn't time to launch many lifeboats. Panic broke out as the fire spread. Before his ship lost the ability to manoeuvre, the captain grounded the *Rigel* on the island of Rosøya. This probably saved the lives of the nearly 300 survivors. Still convinced the ship carried only German troops, the British planes fired on the lifeboats. Norwegians later realised the true nature of the *Rigel*'s cargo, and launched rescue efforts, local doctors working for days to save as many of the injured as they could.

They sank together

The British were also inadvertently responsible for the worst friendly fire incident in history. By the beginning of April 1945 even Germans knew defeat was imminent. Their army was in full retreat, driven back into the fatherland by a now unstoppable Soviet military that had already retaken 1,000 miles of its own conquered territory in the last 18 months. In the remaining concentration camps on the rapidly-shrinking Reich's eastern flank, inmates watched RAF planes fly overhead and knew rescue was getting closer. Head of the SS Heinrich Himmler, who had overseen the machinery of the Holocaust since the beginning, had other ideas. The Russians had liberated Auschwitz in January and Himmler ordered other camps liquidated, the remaining prisoners killed or marched into the heart of Germany, and any trace of what had happened at the sites removed. What remained of Goebbels' propaganda ministry could write off one death camp as a Soviet lie. If the Allies found dozens it would look like policy.

A small fleet of ships were ordered to assemble in the Bay of Lübeck, on the German coast of the Baltic Sea. The civilian vessels included the 2,815-ton passenger ship and freighter *Thielbek*, which had been damaged in an air raid but was ordered to Lübeck before repairs were completed. The 675ft (205m) ocean liner *Cap Arcona* was also in need of repair, her engine turbines having been worn out through constant use ferrying personnel across the Baltic in the previous few weeks. By the time she reached Lübeck the three-funnelled ship, one of the largest vessels in the German merchant navy, had lost most of its manoeuvrability.

The 21,046-ton liner *Deutschland*, meanwhile, had begun conversion to a hospital ship, but the German military had supposedly run out of paint, so the red cross was only painted on one side of the ship.

Their vessels were now under SS jurisdiction, and had been commandeered for a special operation: to transport over 8,000 prisoners in a single journey.

On 17th April the captains of the *Thielbek*, the *Cap Arcona* and another, smaller ship, the *Athen*, were summoned to a conference with the SS. They learnt that their vessels were now under SS jurisdiction, and had been commandeered for a special operation: to transport over 8,000 prisoners between them (and the *Deutschland*) in a single journey. The captain of the *Thielbek* refused and was immediately relieved of his command. The captain of the *Athen* only accepted under threat of capital charges. Only the *Cap Arcona*'s captain accepted his orders without making a fuss. He knew the SS would proceed with the mission anyway and his being shot would make no difference to that. But before he left the meeting he categorically renounced any responsibility for his ship.

The first prisoners reached the Bay of Lübeck on 19th April and began boarding the next day. The death marches across Poland and Germany from the outlying camps in the winter of 1945 had already claimed tens of thousands of lives. Without food and water, shoes, or adequate clothing against sub-zero temperatures, only the knowledge that the Nazis would soon be defeated gave many the determination to carry on. As they were driven into the dark, cold, wet holds of the ships, they didn't know they would have to wait almost two weeks before the last groups of prisoners were crowded aboard and the order for departure received. Most of them were Russian and Polish, but there were prisoners from 28 different nationalities, including Americans, teenage French resistance fighters and German political prisoners. Some had survived five years in various camps, including Auschwitz, so the terrible conditions on board the Nazis' hellships were nothing new. But whilst some prisoners on the *Cap Arcona* were crammed, with only room to stand, into a barely lit storeroom for the ship's provisions, when the holds were full the SS began to fill the rest of the ship too, including the liner's extravagant Victorian banquet hall. Prisoners boarding the ship walked down the main stairwell, which had a beautiful Persian carpet, exquisite mahogany and brass railings, and a brocade tapestry covering the walls.

Some had survived five years in various camps, including Auschwitz, so the terrible conditions on board the Nazis' hellships were nothing new.

On 30th April, Hitler committed suicide. The prisoners in the Bay of Lübeck learnt of it from their guards on 2nd May following new leader Admiral Karl Doenitz's radio address. Naturally, word spread through the ships in a matter of hours, along with (accurate) rumours that the

Red Army had taken control over most of Berlin. But the war wasn't over yet. Unrestricted warfare continued under Doenitz as he tried to engineer it so that Germany would surrender to Britain and the United States rather than the Soviet Union. At 2.30pm on 3rd May, the ships' captains were given the order to leave on their mission. Though the prisoners on board did not know it, British military columns were now only miles from Lübeck.

The RAF was also close to achieving air supremacy over the Baltic. The British policy of attacking all ships, military or otherwise, continued based on intelligence reports that the Germans were using unmarked civilian ships to transport large numbers of troops, SS personnel and key Nazi Party figures to Norway. A surveillance plane flying over the *Cap Arcona* and *Deutschland* reported seeing only soldiers on deck, and had to evade anti-aircraft fire. The ships became a legitimate target.

Only the *Athen* avoided the subsequent attack. Her captain had returned to the quayside to pick up more prisoners. When a squad of Hawker Typhoon bombers began their assault on the ships anchored out in the bay, he ran his vessel into the quay and raised a white flag. Doing so saved the lives of the 1,998 aboard.

For some of the bomber pilots, the raid on the Bay of Lübeck seemed like their last opportunity to take revenge on Nazis whose evil crimes were only now being fully revealed, Bergen-Belsen having been liberated a fortnight before. The pilots, one of whom was Jewish, did not learn of the ships' true cargo for almost thirty years. In an attack that lasted an hour, they scored direct hit after direct hit, over 60 rockets being fired and all of them hitting their stationary targets.

Struck by a combination of rockets, other bombs and machine gun fire, the *Thielbek*, carrying almost 3,000 prisoners, caught on fire and began to list to starboard. She sank before her attackers had completed a second attack run on the *Cap Arcona*, but the waters in the bay were so shallow she did not disappear entirely below the surface. Only 50 survivors escaped before she went down.

Prisoners on the Cap Arcona *began to suspect the Germans were scuttling the ship, intending to slaughter them all and hide the evidence underwater.*

Prisoners on the *Cap Arcona* thought she had been struck by a torpedo at first, but as she was struck again and again, others began to suspect the Germans were scuttling the ship, intending to slaughter them all and hide the evidence underwater. As fire began to spread through the ship and their guards fled, prisoners stampeded through the ship's slanting passageways, not knowing which way to go. People tried to escape up the ship's burning stairwell, but the flames were too widespread, the smoke too thick. Water poured into the ship and the lights went out, but the sirens continued to wail in the darkness. Ropes were lowered into the lavatory block for those trapped on the lower deck to climb up, but in the panic, desperate people pulled at each other and climbed over others, fighting to get up. Only a few were saved before fire swept in minutes later.

As smoke and fire enveloped the top deck, those who managed to make it up there began jumping into the water. They could see the shore, barely 2 miles (3.5km) away. Many thought they could swim it. Plenty of them drowned before they reached the beach, half-starved and weakened by their captivity. For those who made it, massacre awaited. SS personnel rescued from the *Cap Arcona* by German trawlers summarily executed as many as they could, leaving the bodies on the sand to be discovered by the approaching British Army in the next few days.

Those who remained on the *Cap Arcona* found most of the lifeboats damaged beyond use by the attack. When the RAF planes returned for their second attack run on the *Cap Arcona*, they also came with orders to shoot at people trying to escape. Prisoners waved their striped caps in the air and pointed to their striped clothes, but these would only become emblematic later. Despite being fired upon themselves, many cheered the RAF for bombing a German patrol boat. Survivors still waiting on deck as well as those in the water thought it had come to rescue them. Instead it seemed like the helmsman was deliberately running over people in the water to kill them with the propeller. The British pilots thought the boat was trying to rescue survivors so bombed and sank it.

The *Cap Arcona* eventually rolled onto her side and sank, though like the *Thielbek* part of her hull remained above the waterline. She had taken much longer to sink than the *Thielbek*, meaning that most of the estimated 4,500 prisoners who died would have burned to death or been asphyxiated by smoke long before they had a chance to drown. The *Deutschland* took even longer to sink – about four hours – so many managed to escape. A small fishing boat picked up some survivors from the water, leaving them in the shallows to swim ashore whilst returning to save more. In total only 350 prisoners from the *Cap Arcona* survived.

> Less than 24 hours later, Germany surrendered unconditionally.

Less than 24 hours later, Germany surrendered unconditionally. In the jubilation of victory – or for many in Europe, including Germany, simply the relief of peace – the tragedy was quickly forgotten by everyone except survivors and those who lived on the Bay of Lübeck. The locals saw the heads of floating corpses bobbing in the water just offshore for days afterwards, and bodies washed up on the beaches for weeks. Bones were still being found as late as the 1970s.

At a later war crime trial the head of Hamburg's Gestapo revealed that Himmler intended all of those on board the ships to be killed, which added to the speculation that the SS planned to scuttle the ships, and also gave birth to the theory that the Nazis used the Allies to do their dirty work. As with the *Lancastria* sinking, the British government sealed all of its records regarding the disaster for a hundred years.

The *Cap Arcona*'s burnt-out wreck eventually drifted onto the shore, where it was broken up in 1949. That same year both the *Deutschland* and the *Thielbek* were raised. The *Deutschland* was scrapped, but the *Thielbek* was considered salvageable. The human remains found aboard were interred in Neustadt, north of Lübeck, and the ship was repaired and renamed *Reinbek*. Later renamed twice more, first to *Magdalene* and then *Old Warrior*, she sailed under a Panamanian flag until she was finally scrapped in 1974.

War of annihilation

Between 1941 and 1945 Germany and the Soviet Union had fought a war within a war, an ideological conflict marked by unmatched carnage, the essential aim of each side annihilation of the other, and which resulted in the majority of the casualties of the Second World War. An uneasy peace existed between the two nations following the non-aggression pact that saw them both invade Poland in September

Between 1941 and 1945 Germany and the Soviet Union inflicted many of the deadliest maritime disasters in history upon each other.

1939, but after Operation Barbarossa, Hitler's attempted invasion of Russia in June 1941, the former allies began engaging in largely unrestricted warfare on land, in the air and at sea. With naval vessels, troop transports, merchant shipping and hospital ships all considered fair game, over the next four years the two countries inflicted many of the deadliest maritime disasters in history upon each other.

Initially the Russo-German war went very much in Hitler's favour, with nearly 4 million men advancing over 1,000 miles into the Soviet Union, and only being checked at the gates of Moscow by a harsh Russian winter. As the German land forces swept along the coast of the Black Sea in November 1941, the Russian navy conscripted merchant ships to help evacuate personnel from the Crimea. One of these vessels was the *Armenia*, one of the first passenger ships built in the Soviet Union. Despite only having capacity for less than 1,000, up to five times that number may have boarded at Sevastopol for the relatively short voyage across the Black Sea to Tuapse, which was safer from the German advance. However, after leaving Sevastopol, the captain was ordered into Yalta to pick up even more. By the 6th, Yalta had been under siege for a week, all the roads had been cut off, and the city was expected to fall to the Germans within hours. In the panic at the quayside, no names were taken, no heads were counted. As the *Armenia* headed out into the Black Sea, she probably carried between 5,000 and 7,000 people, many of them wounded soldiers, but also refugees, including hospital staff. Doctors in Yalta had urged many of the weakest to get on the ship, and then joined them on her. If contemporary Soviet propaganda was to be believed, the *Armenia* had in excess of 8,000 on board.

Had the ship not stopped at Yalta, the thousands who boarded her at Sevastopol would probably have made it safely to Tuapse. Instead the delay meant she left Yalta as the Luftwaffe secured dominion over the Black Sea's airspace. The *Armenia* was only a few miles from Yalta when a Heinkel He-111 dropped two torpedoes into the water. Eyewitnesses on shore claimed they could still see the red crosses painted on the ship's sides at that distance, so they knew the pilot must have seen them too. The first torpedo missed the *Armenia*, but the second hit her prow. Splitting in two, the ship went down in less than 5 minutes. People on shore heard the explosions and screaming. Most of those on board didn't have time to escape, but many of those on deck jumped overboard and tried to swim back to the shore. Being wounded and weakened, hardly any of them made it. The true death toll will never be known, but there were only 8 survivors.

After the disastrous battle for Stalingrad from summer 1942 to early 1943, the tide of war on the Eastern Front turned against the Germans, and in 1944 another maritime disaster in the Black Sea mirrored the loss of the *Armenia* three years before, and perhaps provided the Russians with a satisfying sense of vengeance. By April 1944 the Red Army had retaken enough territory to cut the Crimea off from the rest of Ukraine, trapping almost a quarter of a million German and Romanian soldiers on the peninsula. On 10th May, the captured Hungarian cargo ship *Totila*, and another vessel, the *Teja*, docked at Khersones, not far from Sevastopol. It's possible over 9,000 soldiers, both German and Romanian, boarded for the voyage across the Black Sea to Constanta, Romania, which was still under Axis control. The Soviet airforce now controlled the skies above the Black Sea, and the ships came under attack from dozens of A-20 planes. Three bombs struck the *Totila*, and she sank fast. Neither the *Teja* nor the ships' escort vessels stopped to pick up survivors because that would make them easy targets. Nevertheless, in the second attack wave the Soviet planes hit the *Teja* anyway, and she also sank quickly. This time the escort vessels did stop, but they only rescued 400.

Operation Hannibal

By January 1945, Admiral Doenitz had accepted that Germany was going to lose the war. Realising that the pace of the Soviet advance on the eastern front would leave millions of Germans cut off, he put Operation Hannibal into effect. Hitler was determined to fight until the end, so Doenitz may have managed to make Operation Hannibal look like a strategic repositioning, not retreating but fortifying the fatherland. Ultimately the operation became the largest evacuation by sea in history, transporting up to 2 million people – more than double the number the British evacuated from Dunkirk, Le Havre and St Nazaire – from the east, across the Baltic, to safer ports deeper inside Germany. For the most part, it was a success, the last success of the military machine that between 1939 and 1941 had seemed unstoppable.

Over 1,000 vessels may have been involved at some stage, from small fishing boats up to luxury liners like the

Operation Hannibal became the largest evacuation by sea in history, transporting more than double the number the British evacuated from Dunkirk.

550ft (168m) *Steuben*. The *Steuben* had sunk once before, in 1930. The first German liner to sail to New York since the end of the First World War, she was docked there in July when a fire broke out in a paint locker, spread to a storage hold and then caused an explosion. Raising and repairing the ship became one of the largest salvage efforts in history. In 1944, having been requisitioned as a troop transport, she carried thousands of men eastward. Less than a year later, on 9th February 1945, she docked at Pillau (now Baltiysk, the westernmost town in Russia) to pick up evacuees heading westward. She had cabin space for 793 but could carry about 1,800. Some 2,800 wounded soldiers boarded her at Pillau, along with at least 1,400 other refugees. Naval officers on board reported only 3,600 passengers, but merchant navy officers helping out claimed there had to be at least 5,200.

The next day, as the *Steuben* passed the Stolpe (now Słupsk) Bank, only 40 miles from the German coast, she came into the sights of Soviet submarine S-13. The Russians fired two torpedoes, which hit her broadside below the bridge and split open her hull. Water rushed in so fast that when divers explored her wreck in 2004 they found everything inside that was loose had been swept away, and fittings had even been torn from the walls. As the *Steuben* sank, the passengers who were able surged toward the stern, hoping the bow would hit the seabed in the shallow waters and that the rear of the ship would stay propped up above the water. Instead the *Steuben* rolled onto her side after less than 20 minutes, sinking too fast for the thousands of injured men on stretchers still waiting below to be carried up on deck. In the near-freezing waters, most of those who had been on deck when she went under did not survive long. Only a few hundred survivors were picked up by an escorting torpedo boat.

> *Water rushed in so fast that when divers explored her wreck they found everything inside that was loose had been swept away, and fittings had even been torn from the walls.*

About 160 vessels participating in Operation Hannibal were sunk between 23rd January and 8th May 1945. The last major loss was that of the *Goya*, a 5,230-ton Norwegian freighter the Germans had seized in 1940. On 16th April, carrying thousands of soldiers and civilians who had fled the Soviet invasion of Danzig (now Gdansk), she was hit by two torpedoes from Russian mine-laying submarine L-3. Her passenger list officially acknowledged 6,100 people being aboard, but it had been another chaotic evacuation, and it's possible a thousand more could have squeezed onto the ship. The *Goya* had a cruising speed of 18 knots, fast enough to evade submarines, but she stopped when another vessel in her convoy developed engine problems just before midnight. The torpedoes caused the unarmoured freighter to split in two, water flooding into her so fast that it prevented most people from making it out during the mere 7 minutes she took to sink. As with the *Steuben*, those who survived the sinking weren't guaranteed rescue. Most died in the icy water before two minesweepers reached the scene, by which time there were again only a few hundred survivors to be pulled up.

The sinking of the *Goya* made few headlines. In Germany, these catastrophic losses, whether at sea or on land, had become almost routine as the Allies pushed in from every direction. In Britain, the United States, the Soviet Union, and across the swathes of Europe the Allies had already liberated, there was little sympathy for the suffering of the enemy – part of the intoxicating effect of imminent glory. But perhaps part of the reason why the *Goya*'s sinking went largely unnoticed at the time, and has been mostly forgotten today, is because it came so soon after another Operation Hannibal disaster, one that dwarfed the *Goya* in terms of loss of life, and which remains the worst maritime disaster of all time.

7 TEN THOUSAND DEAD

The sinking of the *Wilhelm Gustloff*

The *Wilhelm Gustloff* can now be seen as a symbol for Germany's rise and fall under the Third Reich, and not least because she was originally going to be called the *Adolf Hitler*. Hitler himself chose her new name, using the first purpose-built cruise liner of the DAF (Deutsche Arbeitsfront–German Labour Front) to both commemorate and condemn. Gustloff was the German leader of the Swiss Nazi Party, assassinated in 1936 by a Jewish student. The imposing white liner was meant to show both her German passengers and the parts of the world they visited that Nazism wasn't just a political movement, its success an electoral aberration that would eventually be rectified, but that the Nazi creed was an inherent part of the German identity. By martyrising such a prominent anti-Semite as Gustloff, the ship's naming was a further attempt to normalise the Nazis' attitudes towards the Jews. As such it was also a warning of what was to come, but one which of course few heeded.

Wilhelm Gustloff's widow christened the ship herself. Laid down in August 1936, the ship was ready for launch in May 1937. Displacing 25,484 tons, she was 684ft (208.5m) long and 77.5ft (23.6m) across the beam. Across eight decks she had 489 cabins, designed to carry 1,465 passengers, attended to by a crew of 417. There was no class distinction on board the *Wilhelm Gustloff*. The Nazi ideology disdained the class warfare between rich and poor that defined (and inspired) socialism, as they perceived it. Under the auspices of the DAF's subsidiary KdF (Kraft durch Freude – Strength through Joy), the *Wilhelm Gustloff* offered loyal German workers trips to Norway, Portugal and Italy for less than a third of the price of a comparable cruise.

The Nazi propaganda that all passengers were required to sit through might not even have been necessary by that stage. Just being on the ship probably made a positive impression on most.

In the two years before war broke out the *Wilhelm Gustloff* took 65,000 people on 50 voyages. Much of Germany's rural working class had never left their villages before. Now they were being taken around Europe on one of the most beautiful, luxurious ships in the world, treated to concerts, dances and films. The Nazi propaganda that all passengers were required to sit through might not even have been necessary by that stage. Just being on the ship probably made a positive impression on most.

The *Wilhelm Gustloff*'s propaganda role wasn't just aimed at her passengers, though. It was also her job to put an attractive face on Hitler's new, modern Germany and cast doubts on aspersions made in the wake of punitive restrictions against Jews and laws banning opposition parties. In April 1938 the *Wilhelm Gustloff* docked several miles off the British coast to allow German and Austrian citizens living in the United Kingdom to vote in the referendum on Anschluss – whether Austria should be completely absorbed into Germany. Around 2,000 travelled to Tilbury to be ferried to and from the *Wilhelm Gustloff*. Only four of them voted no. The British press reported positively on the magnificent ship anchored near the Thames Estuary, and how the efforts Germany had gone to ensure its citizens overseas could vote showed that the Nazis were not the enemies of liberty some sabre-rattling troublemakers on the Conservative Party's backbenches claimed they were. It was, of course, simply a propaganda exercise, and a fait d'accompli. German troops had occupied Austria a month before.

It certainly didn't hurt the British impression of the *Wilhelm Gustloff* that a week before the Anschluss referendum she had come to the rescue of a British cargo ship. The *Wilhelm Gustloff* had been the closest vessel when the *Pegaway* ran into trouble during heavy weather off Terschelling, northern Netherlands. Responding to the distress signal, the *Wilhelm Gustloff* rescued all 19 crewmembers from the stricken ship. As far as the British press was concerned, this heroic Germany was not the dangerous enemy that the likes of Winston Churchill predicted she would become.

When war ultimately did break out less than 18 months later the *Wilhelm Gustloff* was immediately requisitioned into the Kriegsmarine to serve as a 500-bed hospital ship. In July 1940 she anchored in the English Channel with other support vessels in anticipation of Operation Sea Lion, the planned invasion of Britain. Following the Luftwaffe's failure to knock out the RAF in the Battle of Britain, and Hitler's cancellation of the invasion, she spent four years docked at Gotenhafen (now Gdynia) in occupied Poland, serving as a floating barracks for German naval personnel.

In January 1945, only 12 years into the 1,000-year Reich that Hitler had predicted in 1934, the *Wilhelm Gustloff* was conscripted into Operation Hannibal. Her final voyage symbolises the final chapter in the history of the Third Reich. With the Soviet Union consuming Germany from the east and the British and Americans consuming Germany from the west, the final victims of Hitler's war would be his own people.

'A nice ship to be torpedoed'

The winter of 1945 was the coldest in almost twenty years, but that hadn't stopped nearly 100,000 German refugees travelling through the snow – sometimes for days, often on foot – to reach Gotenhafen on the northern Polish coast. Rumours of Soviet atrocities came in advance of their armies. There were stories of unarmed people being clubbed to death, and of women being raped and then crucified naked on doors. Stories of a Soviet spearhead catching up with a straggling group of fleeing Germans and then making them lie in the snow to be crushed under a tank drove the refugees on faster, through the night and snowstorms, never stopping for long.

Following the joint Russian and German invasion of Poland that ignited the Second World War in 1939, some 1.3 million German civilians had moved into the Reich's newest neighbourhoods. This was Hitler's promise of lebensraum ('living space'). These civilians did not see themselves as occupiers, because there were no Poles left in the areas they moved to. They were settlers on Germany's new frontier. They did not ask where the Poles had gone, and the Nazi propaganda machine certainly did not allow them to find out. Five years later, as the Red Army swept into Poland, these settlers did not see the Soviet invasion as a liberation, but simply as a clash of empires. Most Russians – and most Poles, for that matter – probably saw it the same way.

After the Soviet army surrounded East Prussia, the only escape for Germans trapped behind the Russian side of the new eastern front would be by sea.

When the Soviet army broke through on three fronts on 12th January it wasn't long before East Prussia was surrounded. After that point, the only escape for Germans trapped behind the Russian side of the new eastern front would be by sea. Rumours of big German ships docking at Gotenhafen had spread just as fast as the rumours of Soviet atrocities coming from the other direction. Thousands poured into Gotenhafen and headed for the docks. Though they were exhausted and cold, many waited on the piers, listening to artillery rumble like thunder in the distance, hoping it was their own but suspecting it was not. Many of them would wait there in the snow for several days.

The *Wilhelm Gustloff* had been set aside to carry wounded soldiers and those similarly unfit to continue the fight. This included women with children, boys under the age of 16 and men over the age of 50. Civilian refugees would ultimately constitute the vast majority of the thousands crowded onto the ship, but military personnel, including Nazi officials who had been in Poland to administer the conquered country, were also ordered to evacuate. SS stormtroopers patrolled the dockside even before boarding commenced, searching the crowds for deserters, able-bodied men and even underage boys who could be conscripted into the final defence of the fatherland.

No fewer than four captains had been assigned to the *Wilhelm Gustloff*, which inevitably led to a clash over who was really in command before they even left port. Officially her civilian captain Friederich Petersen was in charge. He knew the ship better than the other three captains, having commanded her briefly in 1938 when, serving as second in command, he had to take over following the sudden death of her captain. Petersen was 67, and had actually been captured by the British earlier in the war. They released him on compassionate grounds, and on the assumption – and indeed, his promise – that he would not return to active service.

No fewer than four captains had been assigned to the Wilhelm Gustloff, which inevitably led to a clash over who was really in command before they even left port.

At 33, Wilhelm Zahn was half Petersen's age, and he had no time for the civilian's claim to command. As far as he was concerned, the *Wilhelm Gustloff*'s mission was a military one. The ship was not going on a cruise, and the operation needed to be run by a captain who knew about evading mines and aircraft. But Zahn's experience was as a U-boat commander. He had never commanded a ship like the *Wilhelm Gustloff*. But with a harsh reputation, and his Alsatian dog Hassan always at his side, Zahn was an overbearing character, and the other two young merchant marine captains on the bridge of the *Wilhelm Gustloff* were successfully cowed by his oppressive approach.

On 25th January boarding began. The first to board were not the poor who had been huddling on the pier for days but the rich who had used their money and connections to ensure they got the pick of the cabins. The soldiers supervising boarding struggled to control the surge of the crowd as the gangways were then opened to everyone else.

In the crush, children were separated from their parents. Some would never see each other again.

Boarding on a first come first served basis, those stuck at the back of a crowd that filled their end of the harbour pressed forward, fearing that a ship like the *Wilhelm Gustloff* could only carry a couple of thousand people. In the crush, children were separated from their parents. Some would never see each other again, even though they all managed to board the ship.

After two days, the soldiers registering every passenger who boarded stopped taking names. There were already 5,000 people on board by that time, but the crowd in Gotenhafen didn't seem to have diminished at all as hundreds more arrived every hour. Boarding continued until the 29th. The cabins had long been filled with more people than they could comfortably house, and now the other areas of the ship that had been cleared and laid out with mats began to fill up too. Mattresses lined the floor of the theatre. Even the swimming pools had been drained, and 400 women were housed in one of them.

On the 29th there was an air raid on Gotenhafen. When the sirens wailed some people left the ship to go to one of the harbour's shelters. Many stayed where they were, knowing they could lose their place aboard to someone more scared of the Soviets than of death. This was not an uncommon opinion. As one passenger reportedly said as she came aboard, the *Wilhelm Gustloff* was 'a nice ship to be torpedoed, but better to drown than to fall into Russian hands.'

Mattresses lined the floor of the theatre. Even the swimming pools had been drained, and 400 women were housed in one of them.

That evening the four captains received the order to depart. The gangways were finally retracted, leaving plenty on the pier, many of them in a state of fear and panic. The last people to come aboard were the Nazi mayor of Gotenhafen and his family. They took the luxury suite that had been reserved solely for Hitler's use, but which had never been occupied in the ship's eight-year lifetime.

A combined passenger list and crew complement recognised there as being only 6,050 on board. In the 1980s and 1990s research concluded that there were actually between 8,956 and 10,582 people on the *Wilhelm Gustloff* when she left Gotenhafen, and that around 4,000 of them were children. Whether the true number was nearer the lower estimate or the higher one, this meant that there may have only been enough lifejackets for about half of those aboard.

'A dog leading an elephant'

The *Wilhelm Gustloff* finally left Gotenhafen at 12.15pm on the 30th, so heavy that it took four tugs to manoeuvre her away from the pier. A lack of escort ships had delayed her departure from the previous evening, the only ones available being small auxiliary vessels of poor seaworthiness, unsuited to an open sea passage. The Kriegsmarine could not spare ships that could match the *Wilhelm Gustloff*'s maximum speed of 15 knots, and it lacked the materials to make repairs to others that were more suitable for escort duties, but which had been damaged by Soviet or British air attacks.

Having to feed over 10,000 people, supplies on the *Wilhelm Gustloff* quickly diminished, so her four captains decided to leave with the escort they had rather than risk the possibility of never being able to leave at all. They were to travel in convoy with another passenger liner, the *Hansa*, which was also full of civilian refugees and military personnel. The convoy also included the whaling boat *Walter Rau* and two torpedo boats, but one of those, the *Lowe*, did not have the latest sonar or radar, and the freezing temperatures had caused her other equipment to seize up too. Another snowstorm descended over the Bay of Danzig as they left its sheltered waters that lunchtime. Zahn, looking out at their insufficient escort, commented to Petersen, 'This looks like a dog leading an elephant into the night.'

Two portentous events occurred before the *Wilhelm Gustloff* made it into the open sea of the Baltic. First she had an impromptu rendezvous with the steamer *Reval*, which had come from Pillau and carried 600 refugees. Unable to take them all the way to Germany, her captain requested the *Wilhelm Gustloff* take them instead. The four captains submitted, and all 600 were transferred to the liner. By this stage her corridors were already impassable.

Shortly after that, the *Hansa* developed mechanical problems and one of the torpedo boats reported a leak. Neither could continue and had to turn back. Zahn in particular had been dismayed by their escort when they left Gotenhafen. Now Petersen and the other captains were also unsure whether it would be safe to continue, effectively alone. But Zahn's dismay did not equate with any degree of willingness to fail his mission. So the *Wilhelm Gustloff* headed out into the Baltic Sea, her course set for Kiel, northern Germany.

This was when Petersen and Zahn had their first truly significant disagreement. Zahn was a submariner and believed the best course to take would be a zigzagging course through shallow waters close to shore. Not only did Soviet submarines avoid shallow waters because it made them easier to find, but in the event that the *Wilhelm Gustloff* was attacked, she could always be run aground, and her more than 10,000 passengers could escape ashore. Petersen, however, feared British aircraft more than Soviet submarines, and most RAF activity was either over land or close to the coast. Zahn was more concerned about Soviet planes, though, which as far as he was aware were flying reconnaissance flights over the Baltic. A coastal course, therefore, would hopefully avoid the Soviet threat altogether.

Ultimately Zahn's recalcitrance failed to sway either Petersen or the other merchant marine captains, and the *Wilhelm Gustloff* continued along a deep-water course that had been swept for mines. The captains ordered the ship's anti-aircraft armaments (of which the *Wilhelm Gustloff* had three 105mm guns and eight 20mm cannons) to be kept at a constant state of readiness. This was easier said than done for the crewmen who had to struggle across the icy decks in a mounting blizzard to repeatedly clear the frozen weapons.

Running into trouble out at sea, with help far away, would leave the ship a sitting duck.

Zahn also urged Petersen to push the engines to their limits. At a maximum speed of 15 knots, the *Wilhelm Gustloff* could outrun most submarines. Though Petersen refused, he had good reason to. The liner had been docked at Gotenhafen for the better part of four years, in which time her engines had not been run at all. Not only did running her engines at top speed risk causing them to break down, but it also risked reopening a gash in the hull that the ship had received from an earlier explosion whilst in port. Makeshift welding ensured she was sufficiently seaworthy for this trip, but not without limitation. Petersen knew why the captain of the *Hansa* had turned back rather than risk the journey. Running into trouble out at sea, with help far away, would leave the ship a sitting duck, and they would stand little chance against either the Soviets or the British, whichever found them first. What's more,

the *Wilhelm Gustloff*'s hull had not received any anti-
fouling treatments for a long time. Encrusted with
barnacles, she would struggle to make 15 knots. As it was,
the most she managed on her final voyage was 12 knots, a
speed at which she might have struggled to outrun
submarines.

The weather grew steadily worse as evening approached.
The snowstorm became thicker and visibility dropped
almost to zero, which brought mixed blessings – on the
one hand, the *Wilhelm Gustloff* was harder to spot; on the
other, so were her enemies. The four captains ordered each
lookout watch to be increased to eight men.

Sailing into darkness with her lights off, the *Wilhelm
Gustloff* received an odd radio message. Atmospheric
interference caused by the bad weather made it difficult to
receive and accurately decode long
distance radio messages, but the
four captains took the message at
face value. Apparently there was a
minesweeper heading along the
same course, but in the opposite
direction, and she would intercept the liner shortly.
However, the source of the radio message could not be
ascertained. Zahn ordered that the ship's navigation lights
be turned on, an order Petersen quickly countermanded.
But this time he would not get his way. The other captains
were as concerned about the risk of collision as Petersen
had been about the risk of driving the engines too hard,
and they supported Zahn. Red running lights lit up the
Wilhelm Gustloff's port side, green her starboard. They
not only made her easier to spot in the dark and amidst the

The weather grew steadily worse as evening approached. The snowstorm became thicker and visibility dropped almost to zero.

blizzard, but they gave away her size and her course too. By the time the captains reached a point where they should have passed the minesweeper, realised she didn't actually exist and turned the navigation lights off again, it was already too late.

They had also received another radio warning but felt far enough away from the danger to ignore it. Soviet submarine movements had been decoded, and there were supposedly three submarines patrolling the Bay of Danzig. That was where they had come from, and Zahn knew the Russian vessels were too far behind to catch up with them now. What he didn't know was that one of the submarines, S-13, commanded by Captain Alexander Marinesko, had left the others behind hours before, and by chance alone was now only a few miles from the *Wilhelm Gustloff*.

'This is it'

Below decks, the *Wilhelm Gustloff*'s passengers were suffering. The temperature may have dropped to −17°C (5°F) outside, driven by a Force 7 gale, but inside the ship the sheer number of people squeezed onto her eight decks created a hot and increasingly humid atmosphere. Those with lifejackets had been ordered over the ship's loudspeakers to wear them at all times, but many removed them because it was so hot. Facilities designed to cater for fewer than 2,000 people struggled to cope with more than five times as many, not least the 145 toilets,

As Hitler ranted, a baby was born in the belly of the ship.

which quickly became blocked. It didn't help that the rough seas made thousands of people seasick. Foul odours permeated through the corridors, where hundreds sat and lay on the floor because there was no room for them anywhere else. Meanwhile, upbeat music was played over the loudspeakers.

The 30th January was the twelfth anniversary of the day Hitler became Chancellor of Germany. To commemorate the occasion he gave a speech calling upon every German to rise up and resist the Jewish Communist plot to destroy Germany before it was too late. In the end it turned out to be the last radio speech he made. At 8pm a recording was played over the *Wilhelm Gustloff*'s loudspeakers. The refugees listened to it because there was nothing else to do, but gone were the days when Hitler's triumphalist rhetoric inspired an almost hysterical reaction. On the bridge, officers joked that they would happily switch it off, but didn't want the hassle from the Gestapo. As Hitler ranted, a baby was born in the belly of the ship.

The speech lasted about an hour, at the end of which Zahn and the other captains headed to Petersen's cabin for dinner – hot pea soup. The cooks and stewards worked round the clock, because by the time one group had been fed, it was time to feed another. The ship's passages were so crowded it made it difficult for stewards to reach everyone with soup, sandwiches, porridge and other basic rations. But their tallies of the number of people that needed feeding gave the captains their most accurate estimation of the number aboard, and, including those too seasick to eat, the figure was at the upper end of all the estimates.

Now that they had turned the navigation lights off again, the four dining captains felt as good as invisible in the dark and in the constant snow. They were fatally mistaken.

The Soviet submarine S-13 had been stalking the *Wilhelm Gustloff* for over an hour. Her petty officer had been on watch duty when he spotted the liner's navigation lights. The blizzard and the big seas could have hidden the ship from the S-13's periscope view, but her lights shone like a beacon in the darkness. Indeed, the Russians initially mistook the *Wilhelm Gustloff* for a lighthouse, and only on consulting their charts did they realise it was a ship. Just after 9pm, her lights now off, the *Wilhelm Gustloff* was about 19 miles (30km) off the Polish coast, near the Stolpe Bank. The S-13's Captain Marinesko ordered his crew to surface on the ship's port side, on the assumption that the liner's lookouts would be paying more attention to dangers from seaward. Slowly, unnoticed, the Soviet submarine closed to 3,000ft (less than 1km).

In the panicked silence of the following moments, passengers throughout the ship's crowded cabins and corridors wondered what they had hit.

Four torpedoes were primed and ready to fire. Marinesko gave the order. Three launched successfully. The fourth jammed in its tube. Most of the S-13's crew were too busy trying to disarm it to take any notice of their target's fate.

The first torpedo struck the *Wilhelm Gustloff* near the bow, level with the bridge. Everybody on the ship would have heard the thunderous roar. In the panicked silence of the following moments, passengers throughout the ship's crowded cabins and corridors wondered what they had hit. Many assumed it was a mine. The emergency fire bells started ringing immediately, but for most there was nowhere to go, not until everyone between them and the stairs moved first.

Then the second torpedo struck, and after that there was no mistaking the fact that the ship was under attack. The torpedo hit near midship, blasting a hole in the hull just above the drained swimming pools. The explosion killed many of the women housed there instantly. The torrent of freezing seawater that followed killed the rest.

The third torpedo hit the *Wilhelm Gustloff* just as the senior officer on the bridge was ordering an emergency stop. It struck the hull below the ship's single funnel. From the Russians' perspective, this was their most successful torpedo. It scored a direct hit on the engine room. In an instant, the *Wilhelm Gustloff* lost all power. Her internal lights blinked off, plunging thousands of terrified passengers into darkness. The ringing of the fire bells and the constant hum of the ship's systems was replaced by deathly silence, broken only by the screams and shouts of those trapped inside the bowels of the ship. The emergency generators quickly activated, but the dim red emergency lights would only have been bright enough to show most people just how difficult it would be to escape such an overcrowded ship.

By the time the four captains made it onto the bridge, the *Wilhelm Gustloff* was already settling by the head and listing slightly to port. Both Petersen and Zahn knew immediately that the ship was doomed. 'Das ist es,' Petersen muttered. *This is it*. He knew as well as Zahn how many people they had aboard, and he knew that with the ship foundering so fast, most of them would die. He took the decision to close all the bow bulkheads. Doing so slowed the water's progress and gave people more time to try and escape. Despite this, it was not an easy or obvious decision to make. After all, sleeping in their bow quarters at the time of the attack were most of the crewmembers who were trained in how to launch the lifeboats. Closing the bulkheads not only condemned them to death, but ensured everyone else aboard would have to fend for themselves too.

Dead in the water

Finding the line to the engine room dead, Zahn accepted the futility of hoping to restore power to send a distress signal. The emergency generator provided insufficient power to send long-distance messages, so Zahn used a spotlight to contact the torpedo boat *Lowe*, which was 15 minutes away. The crew of the *Lowe* received the sobering news that the *Wilhelm Gustloff* would sink within the hour, and dutifully carried out Zahn's instructions.

It quickly became apparent that regardless of who came to the rescue, they would probably arrive too late.

They sent the SOS that the sinking liner could not, requesting immediate assistance and directing all available ships to hurry to the *Wilhelm Gustloff*'s aid. Then the *Lowe*'s captain followed those directions himself.

Back on the *Wilhelm Gustloff*, the crew began to fire red distress rockets. They had little to lose from giving away their position now. Perhaps even enemy vessels would take pity on the thousands of souls aboard her. It quickly became apparent to Petersen and Zahn, however, that regardless of who came to the rescue, they would probably arrive too late.

Below decks, dust and the smell of explosive filled the air. Panic took hold as soon as the torpedoes struck, not least in the cabins, where those with beds had managed to get to sleep until the blasts shocked them awake. Stirring to the roar of rushing water (described by one survivor as sounding like Niagara Falls), some found they couldn't open their cabin doors. It wasn't simply a problem of fumbling in pitch darkness. The explosions had caused some doorframes to buckle, jamming the doors shut. Shrieking and hammering on the doors, passengers managed to draw the attention of people on the other side, who broke the doors open with fire axes.

As the *Lowe* drew alongside the *Wilhelm Gustloff*, the torpedo boat's captain and crew could see how badly the liner was now listing to port. Hundreds were pouring up onto the top deck every minute, finding it doubly hard to walk on the increasingly tilted deck because it was already iced over. The *Lowe* took as many as she could, until it was standing room only and she was even more crowded than the *Wilhelm Gustloff*. People had to swim a short distance through the freezing water to reach the torpedo boat. Once aboard they were taken down to the engine room to warm up, stripped of their clothes and given blankets. Crewmen on the *Lowe* even surrendered articles of their own clothing to some of the naked, shivering survivors.

The *Lowe* pulled away, to the despair of those still amassing on the *Wilhelm Gustloff*'s top deck. They had reason to cheer, however, when another vessel came into sight. The lookouts of heavy cruiser *Admiral Hipper* had witnessed the torpedo attack on the *Wilhelm Gustloff* and her crew had picked up the *Lowe*'s proxy SOS. The *Admiral Hipper* gave the *Wilhelm Gustloff*'s passengers good reason to believe they were saved. Having survived nearly six years of naval warfare, she was now the largest German warship in the Baltic Sea. But she was already carrying 1,500 evacuees herself. She could reach speeds of 32 knots, more than enough to escape submarines. Fearing that stopping to help the *Wilhelm Gustloff* would put them in danger, the *Admiral Hipper*'s captain called off the approach and ordered the helmsman to continue to Kiel. On the frozen deck of the *Wilhelm Gustloff*, a thousand people watched the warship disappear into the night.

People found themselves stepping on the dead, unable to resist the surge forward without risking being trampled underfoot themselves.

Inside the doomed liner, the emergency lighting was beginning to fail. The crush on the stairs became lethal as thousands of people jammed the stairwells. People found themselves stepping on the dead, unable to resist the surge forward without risking being trampled underfoot themselves. Desperate people grabbed at each other, reaching for the ankles of those above them to try and pull themselves up. The sound of water below, and of drowning people trapped at the bottom of the stairwells, drove people on. Families were separated in the chaos, some never to see their relatives again. Those who fought their way out of the upward surge to go and search for their loved ones would spend the rest of their lives futilely fighting their way along dark passageways, perhaps only realising too late that they should never have left the stairs.

Meanwhile, in the salon, the majestic grand piano that had never been removed during the *Wilhelm Gustloff*'s years of military service slowly started to roll across the floor.

No escape

The *Wilhelm Gustloff* should have had 22 lifeboats, but 10 were missing. They had been removed in Gotenhafen, some being used in harbour to create a smokescreen that would conceal the mass evacuation from any British or Soviet reconnaissance planes flying over. In their place the *Wilhelm Gustloff* had untethered rafts, positioned on the sundeck and disused tennis courts where they would simply float up if the ship sank. At the time she was torpedoed the *Wilhelm Gustloff* only had enough lifesaving equipment for half of those aboard. But even if the ship had had a full complement of lifeboats, it wouldn't have guaranteed any more would have been saved – as the *Wilhelm Gustloff* listed ever more to port, the lifeboats on that side of the ship became unusable anyway.

At the time she was torpedoed the Wilhelm Gustloff *only had enough lifesaving equipment for half of those aboard.*

In the hurry to let passengers on board and depart Gotenhafen, no boat drills had been carried out. After departure, the sheer number of people aboard made such exercises impractical. With the crewmembers trained in launching the boats trapped in the flooding bow, nobody on deck knew what they were doing. Zahn ordered his own submariners to take up the mantle, but when they struggled across the slippery deck to reach the lifeboats, they found the launching mechanisms frozen solid beneath inches of ice. The men had to hammer the lifeboats free from the davits, but behind them came the surge of panicking passengers. Armed soldiers tried to hold them back and prevent hundreds storming each lifeboat. They called for only women and children to come forward, and for the men to get out of the way. Some of the soldiers realised they would soon be counting themselves amongst the men who were left on the ship when all the lifeboats were gone. One submariner even fired a warning shot at an officer who abandoned the operation and got into a boat himself.

Launching the boats grew increasingly difficult. One was overloaded with almost 100 people and the lines snapped, throwing everyone into the water. Another reached the water but the frozen ropes couldn't be untied. The lifeboat was bound to the sinking ship. Luckily a 10-year-old boy on board had stolen his uncle's *The anti-aircraft guns installed on the deck broke loose. They crashed over the side of the ship and smashed into a lifeboat.* knife before fleeing to Gotenhafen harbour, and the crewmen on the boat used it to cut themselves free. As the ship's list steepened, the anti-aircraft guns installed on the deck broke loose. They crashed over the side of the ship and smashed into a lifeboat. Meanwhile one of those untethered rafts careened down the icy deck and swept a large number of people into the sea as it plummeted overboard.

The last lifeboat was lowered just before 10pm. It carried approximately 80 women and children, but thousands more children remained on board. As the *Wilhelm Gustloff*'s stern rose higher and higher out of the water, people lost their footing and slid off the frozen deck and into the sea. Thinking the ship was about to go under, many started jumping overboard too. They would only have survived a few minutes flailing in the freezing water. Consequently, it is likely that over a thousand people died, floating near the ship, before she even sank.

Many of those still inside the ship seemed to have a good idea that they were not going to make it, and plenty gave up trying. Survivors later reported seeing a hysterical woman chanting to herself, whilst some of the ship's officers enjoyed a cognac brought to them by the head steward.

The *Wilhelm Gustloff*'s promenade deck was enclosed behind glass. The crowds on the wrong side of the glass had to watch the lifeboats being lowered on the other side. But when all the lifeboats were gone, senior officers feared that letting thousands more up onto the upper deck would make the ship top heavy and risked causing an immediate capsize. So they ordered the exits from the promenade deck blocked. Those at the back of the crowd would never find out why they were no longer moving. Those on the starboard side of the promenade deck tried to smash the glass, but it was an inch thick and didn't shatter. Those on the port side watched the water rise up on the other side of the glass and began to panic even more.

Petersen and Zahn stayed on the bridge of the *Wilhelm Gustloff* almost until the end. When it became apparent that her terminal list would soon reach the point where inertia would tip her the rest of the way, they decided to save themselves.

Only moments before she began her death roll, power inexplicably returned to the *Wilhelm Gustloff*. Her lights blinked on again, and to those who had grown accustomed to the dim emergency lighting, it appeared like they shone brighter than ever before. Her

To the thousands still on deck, it felt like a great wave breaking over the ship. Many were swept into the sea.

fire bells also began to ring again, with what seemed like a desperate urgency.

Survivors in the lifeboats watched the magnificent cruise liner slide onto her port side, slowly, almost gracefully. To the thousands still on deck, it felt like a great wave breaking over the ship. Many were swept into the sea, but there were still people standing on the side of the ship's funnel as she finally sank, bow first, straight down, less than an hour after she had been attacked.

The forgotten tragedy

Thousands of people struggled in the freezing water amidst a field of debris and leaked oil. Some had tried to swim away from the *Wilhelm Gustloff* in her last moments, aware that she would create a downdraught that could suck them under. But in every direction there were just more people, living and dead. Many couldn't swim – women, children and people who had spent their entire lives in rural areas, so never learnt. A couple of children grabbed onto a stranger, and rather than kick them off to save himself he swam over to a lifeboat. The occupants lifted the children inside, but there was no room for him. Some of the rafts designed to carry 60 already carried 90. They had to beat off desperate people who threatened to swamp the boats. Others resigned themselves to the fact that there wasn't room for them in the boats, and just clung to the sides to await rescue. It was hard to row the boats through all the people in the water, especially when those people were dead children floating upside down, drowned by lifejackets that were not designed for use by someone so small.

As happened following the loss of the *Titanic*, the majority of those who died survived the sinking but then succumbed to exposure. In the freezing waters, hypothermia set in within minutes. Most were dead within 10. But the harsh winter weather didn't just kill those in the water. With an air temperature between −17°C (5°F) and −10°C (14°F), those in the boats without adequate clothing began to succumb to exposure too. The blizzard continued, covering them with snow, and rough seas splashing water into the lifeboats meant nobody could stay dry either. When rescue ships began to arrive in the middle of the night, they found plenty of corpses in the boats as well as in the water. Most of the survivors of the *Wilhelm Gustloff* were young, fit sailors.

When rescue ships began to arrive in the middle of the night, they found plenty of corpses in the boats as well as in the water.

Minesweepers, torpedo boats, a freighter and other civilian craft reached the site of the sinking by dawn, but by then they were too late. The *Lowe*'s several hundred survivors represented almost half of everyone rescued. Seven hours after the *Wilhelm Gustloff* sank, a patrol boat discovered the last survivor – a one-year-old boy wrapped in a blanket on a lifeboat otherwise filled with snow-covered corpses. Orphaned by the catastrophe, he was later adopted by the sailor who found him. Of the 4,000 children estimated to have been on board the ship when she sank, only 100 survived the disaster.

The remains of the dead continued to wash up on the shores of the Swedish mainland and islands throughout the spring and summer of 1945. As with the sinkings of the *Goya* and the *Steuben*, the news was suppressed in Germany to prevent a loss of morale, and to help the Nazi propagandists promote Operation Hannibal as an unequivocal success. Soviet propaganda, meanwhile, told the Russian people that the *Wilhelm Gustloff* had been transporting SS personnel who worked in the concentration camps. The sinking came only days after the Red Army liberated Auschwitz, after all.

All four captains survived the disaster, but the official naval inquiry only investigated the responsibility of the sole military commander aboard – Wilhelm Zahn. The inquiry was still on-going when the war ended in May, and following the collapse of the Nazi regime, was never resolved.

The man ultimately responsible for the sinking went on to be awarded the highest honour possible – Hero of the Soviet Union. Though Alexander Marinesko had been dead almost 30 years by the time he received it. He was only 32 when he sank the *Wilhelm Gustloff*, a rebellious young commander with a taste for alcohol (which ultimately caused his fatal ulcer in 1963) who was almost court martialled once, and who later went on to spend years in a gulag for insubordination. His war did not end with the destruction of the *Wilhelm Gustloff*, however. Just over a week later the S-13 also sank the *Steuben* (see chapter six).

The man ultimately responsible for the sinking went on to be awarded the highest honour possible.

In 2002 the Nobel Prize-winning author Gunter Grass published *Crabwalk*, in which the sinking of the *Wilhelm Gustloff* is central to a plot that spans fifty years and multiple generations all affected by the disaster in different ways. Grass remains most well-known for his 1959 novel *The Tin Drum*, about an infantilised Germany failing to face up to its actions. He revisited the theme in *Crabwalk*, exploring how the modern Far Right in Germany claimed the *Wilhelm Gustloff* as a symbol of German suffering during the war. Indeed, an internet search about the ship will eventually lead to websites run by Far Right extremists in Germany and the United States. They argue that had Germany sunk a ship carrying over 10,000 British or American civilians then those responsible would have been prosecuted for war crimes, yet nobody was prosecuted for the bombing of Dresden, Hiroshima and Nagasaki, or the sinking of the *Wilhelm Gustloff*, as if glory brought with it immunity. In *Crabwalk*, Grass turns the argument against the Far Right, arguing that they practice the resentment of victimhood because it absolves them of any responsibility.

The wreck of the *Wilhelm Gustloff* lies 144ft (44m) below the surface, designated a war grave by the Polish government and accorded the protection of a ban on divers visiting the site. Her mid-section, where she received the three fatal blows, appears crushed, but her bow and stern remain in comparatively good condition.

8

WORSE THAN *TITANIC*

Maritime disasters since the Second World War

The end of the Second World War didn't bring peace to all of the Pacific. China had been embroiled in civil war for a decade before the Japanese invasion in 1937, and, despite combined efforts to drive Japan out lasting until 1945, once China was free again, the communist and nationalist forces resumed their fight for control of the country. By the end of 1948, the communist faction was closing on Shanghai, and coming nearer to securing absolute victory. People fled Shanghai in their thousands, taking steamships to the relative safety of Chekiang (now Zhejiang) Province, several hundred miles further to the south.

About 2,150 passengers were listed on the manifest of the 2,100-ton steamship *Kiangya*. People had queued for days to buy tickets on any ship leaving the Yangtze River, and desperate demand greatly exceeded limited supply. Spotting an opportunity, the *Kiangya*'s officers decided to ignore the vessel's official capacity of only 1,186. But by allowing such overcrowding they lost control over the actual number who boarded. Some people on board threw their tickets to friends they spotted on the wharf, so whilst their tickets were used twice, they were only counted once. Over 1,000 people may have got on board without a ticket at all. When she finally began steaming towards the open sea on 4th December, it is possible there were between 4,000 and 5,000 people aboard.

The ship shook violently. Terrified passengers on deck saw a column of dirty water rise above the wrecked stern like a geyser.

The *Kiangya* reached the mouth of the river at around 6.30pm. As she moved out into the East China Sea her stern suddenly exploded with an ear-splitting crack. The ship shook violently. Terrified passengers on deck saw a column of dirty water rise above the wrecked stern like a geyser. Inside the ship, the lights went out. Panicking, screaming people pushed and shoved to get out, but the ship was too tightly packed, and began listing rapidly toward the stern. Some escaped by climbing out of cabin windows, but for most people trapped below decks, there wasn't time to get out. Those not killed by the explosion were quickly overcome by the sudden surge of water. There wasn't time to launch many lifeboats either, and some of those that did get away were swamped and sunk by too many people climbing in.

Only minutes after the explosion, the *Kiangya* sank stern-first. The river was shallow, so when the keel hit the riverbed, the *Kiangya*'s superstructure remained suspended above the surface. Over a thousand survivors thrashed in the freezing water, and there wasn't enough room for all of them to climb onto the superstructure, where in places the water would only come up to their waists. The explosion had destroyed the *Kiangya*'s radio, so no SOS had been sent. The 700 survivors had to wait over three hours until other vessels began to arrive and took them back to shore.

Speculation as to the cause of the disaster ranged from the possibility that carrying so many people overworked the *Kiangya*'s boilers, to the generally accepted explanation that the steamship had hit a mine planted by the Japanese navy during the war. But many people in Shanghai, and supporters of the nationalist faction throughout China, refused to believe either story. Instead they believed the suspicions of some members of the *Kiangya*'s crew, who alleged that communists had planted explosives on the ship. Eight years later this version of events still held considerable sway in China, so the now victorious communist government raised the ship. Their subsequent propaganda claimed to prove the *Kiangya* had hit a mine.

The Western reaction to the loss of the *Kiangya* is quite representative of how some of the worst disasters of the post-war era have become little more than a footnote to recent maritime history. The catastrophe made few headlines. Parochial Europe and the United States were still licking their own war wounds, some of which had resulted in casualties that dwarfed those of the *Kiangya*. Perhaps more importantly, and more tellingly, the steamship had sunk on the other side of the world. No Europeans or Americans had been killed. It was a foreign news story. That approach continues to this day, so that even when some of the deadliest maritime disasters of all time have occurred over the past thirty years, they seemed to warrant little attention from the Western world.

Heading home for Christmas

The *Himeyuri Maru* was built in Hiroshima, Japan, and launched in April 1963. Just over 300ft (91.4m) long and 45ft (13.7m) across the beam, she could reach speeds of up to 18 knots. A 2,600-ton passenger ferry, she was capable of carrying about 600 people. In 1975 her owners Onomichi Zosen sold her to Sulpicio Lines in the Philippines. They renamed her the *Don Sulpicio*, and increased the passenger capacity to nearly 1,500. After a fire in 1981, Sulpicio Lines refitted the ship and gave her another new name: the *Doña Paz*. She went on to suffer the worst maritime disaster in living memory.

Twice a week the *Doña Paz* travelled the route from Tacloban City to Manila, the capital of the Philippines, nearly 400 miles away. At around 6.30am on 20th December 1987 she left Tacloban with, according to official records, a full complement of 1,493 passengers. In truth, she was probably carrying three times as many. This was the *Doña Paz*'s last trip before Christmas, and thousands of people wanted to reach loved ones in Manila for the holiday. Entire families travelled together. While the shipping line only had a finite number of tickets, the *Doña Paz* didn't stop taking passengers on board until it was standing room only.

At about 8pm the day before, the oil tanker MT *Vector* had left Limay, Bataan, en route to Masbate, over 200 miles away. She carried a cargo of 8,800 barrels of gasoline, diesel and kerosene. Her operation licence had expired and her master was not properly qualified. She didn't even have a proper lookout on board.

On the bridge of the Doña Paz *a lone apprentice crewmember monitored the ship's progress.*

By 10.30pm on the 20th, most of the passengers on the *Doña Paz* who could sleep were doing so. The ship being so overcrowded, people slept several to a single cot. Some of those without a bed slept in the open air. Throughout the ship's three decks people filled the corridors. Some had brought mats to sit or lie on because they knew how packed the ship would be. It was difficult to move around, but most didn't need to. They expected to arrive at Manila's port in the early hours of the next morning, ready to meet their waiting relatives.

Meanwhile on the bridge of the *Doña Paz* a lone apprentice crewmember monitored the ship's progress. Other officers took advantage of the benign summer sailing conditions to sit down with a beer and watch some television. The captain was watching a video.

Nobody who witnessed the collision survived to explain to investigators how it happened. None of the *Doña Paz*'s 60 crew were rescued, and the only two survivors from the *Vector* both claimed to have been asleep at the time. At around 10.30pm both ships passed Dumali Point on the

Tablas Strait. Given their respective courses (the *Vector* heading eastward, the *Doña Paz* heading north), and the fact that the *Vector*'s hull suffered such a catastrophic breach, it is more than likely that the *Doña Paz* struck the starboard side of the *Vector* with her bow. This does not mean the *Doña Paz* was necessarily at fault, however, because whilst there are no 'right of way' laws of the sea, it is generally accepted that the vessel on the left (the *Vector* in this case) should give way.

The sea on fire

Several thousand sleeping passengers on board the *Doña Paz* awoke in a panic. On the lower decks of the ship nobody knew what had happened, but the impact felt and sounded like an explosion. Two things happened in quick succession which ensured most of the people on board both the *Doña Paz* and the *Vector* would not get off the ships alive: the *Doña Paz* suffered a power failure that plunged the ferry into darkness, and the *Vector*'s ruptured hull began to leak copious quantities of burning oil into the waters around both vessels.

The few survivors who made it out from the lower decks of the *Doña Paz* reported the chaos fuelled by terror as thousands of people in the hopelessly overcrowded belly of the ship tried to find a way up and out in complete darkness. Nobody could see anything, and nobody could give instructions to the surge of people trying to push in every direction at once because of the constant screaming.

Two things happened in quick succession which ensured most of the people on board both the Doña Paz *and the* Vector *would not get off the ships alive.*

Not that the crew of the *Doña Paz* co-ordinated an evacuation. None of the survivors saw or heard any crewmembers giving orders to help people escape. The lockers containing lifejackets remained locked – a precaution previously intended to prevent them from being stolen. Invariably there weren't enough for everyone on board, anyway.

The fire had spread on to the Doña Paz and her wooden lifeboats could not be launched into the burning waters below.

Those from below who made it up to the top deck discovered the true horror of the unfolding disaster. No lifeboats were being launched. It was impossible to do so. Whilst the fire probably started on the *Vector*, the oil slick had now spread so far so quickly that it looked like the sea itself was aflame. The fire had spread on to the *Doña Paz* and her wooden lifeboats could not be launched into the burning waters below.

Though oil tankers like the *Vector* had been designed so that their cargo holds would not explode, the ship had become a raging inferno. Flames spread rapidly through the *Doña Paz* too. Her lower decks, where thousands were already trapped by darkness, filled with smoke. Those who still managed to escape from below recalled not being able to see anything but flames. They may have put it down to God's mercy that they survived, but luck certainly played a part. There were no means to fight a major fire aboard the *Doña Paz*, least of all an oil-based fire that spread as quickly as fuel spilled.

Only 24 people on board the *Doña Paz* when she collided with the *Vector* survived, and most of them suffered horrific burns. With the lifeboats unusable, fire spreading quickly through the ship and no rescue vessels forthcoming, there was only one way off the *Doña Paz*.

A point came when the burning oil had spread so far that it was impossible for anyone to swim far enough without needing to come up for air.

All of those who survived the disaster jumped off the ship and into the burning waters. Hundreds of people attempted it. Most failed. Not only did they have to survive the leap through the flames but they then had to hold their breath long enough to swim under the burning oil slick on the surface. A point came when the burning oil had spread so far that it was impossible for anyone to swim far enough without needing to come up for air. Those who managed it were heavily outnumbered by the charred bodies of those who hadn't.

The unknown dead

The *Doña Paz* sank in 1,800ft (550m) of water at around 12.30am, roughly two hours after the collision, and the *Vector* went down a further two hours after that. It wasn't until after 6am that morning, when the *Doña Paz* was now several hours overdue in Manila, that the Filipino maritime authorities learned of the disaster. It took yet another eight hours for a proper search and rescue operation to be launched, by which time it was mostly too late anyway.

Other vessels in the vicinity of the Tablas Strait responded to the distress calls from the stricken ships, but these small merchant vessels would have been even less capable of tackling the inferno than the crews of the *Doña Paz* and the *Vector* themselves. Arriving on the scene as the ships sank, the merchant ships pulled 26 survivors from the water: the two crewmen from the *Vector* who had slept through the collision, and the 24 passengers who had survived jumping from the decks of the *Doña Paz*. Another passenger ship, the *Don Eusebio*, which would have been big enough to take on board a large number of survivors, circled the area for seven hours, but found nobody else alive.

Officially the death toll of the *Doña Paz*'s sinking still stands at 1,749. Initially the shipping line maintained the ship's manifest was accurate, and that there were only 1,493 passengers and 60 crew aboard when she collided with the *Vector*. However, it quickly became apparent that there were many people unaccounted for, not least young children, who had not been listed on the manifest at all.

Even the generally accepted figure of 4,375 deaths remains an estimate. Investigators came to this number based on the claims of those who reported they had friends or family members sailing from Tacloban to Manila on board the *Doña Paz*. Of course, this figure would not necessarily include those who were travelling with their entire family, or alone, or who had not told anyone where, when and how they were going.

Only 270 bodies washed up on the shores of the Tablas Strait. While the Strait is notorious for being rife with man-eating hammerhead sharks, there are no confirmed reports of either survivors or corpses being attacked, despite the popular theory. The more likely reason why so few bodies were recovered is because the rest went down with the ship.

Of the 21 bodies picked up in the immediate aftermath of the disaster, only one person was identified as having been on the official manifest.

Most people probably died trapped in the dark, overcrowded lower decks of the *Doña Paz*, overcome either by smoke or flames, and unable to make it up top to try and jump and swim to survive.

The true number killed aboard the *Doña Paz* will never be known and may in fact be considerably higher than the 4,375 estimate. After all, of the 21 bodies picked up in the immediate aftermath of the disaster, only one person was identified as having been on the official manifest.

Eye of the storm

Haiti's first democratically elected president, Jean-Bertrand Aristide, held office for only nine months in 1991 before the military staged a coup, objecting to Aristide's attempts to put them under civilian authority. Over the next three years, pro-democracy fighters struggled against the CIA-trained military junta, unrest that led to the deaths of several thousand men, women and children, and which caused tens of thousands to try and flee to the United States. The US Coast Guard patrolled Caribbean waters, seizing control of vessels attempting to reach America, destroying them, and returning those aboard to Haiti. Throughout February 1993, the owners of the 148ft (45m) coastal ferry *Neptune* feared the ship might be hijacked by desperate refugees, so they cancelled her weekly trip from remote parts of western Haiti to the capital, Port-au-Prince, several weeks in a row. So when they finally agreed to let her sail, on 17th February, there was massive demand for tickets.

The *Neptune* was a rusty, rickety triple-deck ferry, built in 1954 and intended as a cargo ship. She had an authorised capacity of only a few hundred, plus 10 crew, but she rarely arrived in Port-au-Prince with less than 650 aboard. Neither the crew nor officials along the *Neptune*'s route kept lists of those who boarded, but they admitted to frequently ignoring any suggested limits, just filling the decks until they were standing room only. Photos taken of the crowded ferry arriving in the capital on previous journeys showed people clinging to the side or perched on deck awnings. Sometimes there were up to 2,000 aboard. A military official supervising loading of cargo (charcoal, coffee, fruit and livestock) at Jeremie, one of the ports along the route, later said that when she left for the last time, he had never seen the *Neptune* look so crowded. Many of the passengers were merchants or students, but others were on their way to Port-au-Prince for the annual carnival.

The Neptune *was now severely imbalanced and top heavy.*

Several hours into the journey, hugging the coastline around Haiti's southern peninsula, the *Neptune* ran into a bad storm. At about 11pm, about halfway to Port-au-Prince, the storm suddenly worsened. Driving rain and rough seas caused the ferry to take on water. Panicking, passengers poured up from below decks, gathering on the open upper deck. The *Neptune* was now severely imbalanced and top heavy. The captain wasn't the only one to notice the ferry start to rock as hundreds of passengers moved from one side to the other to escape the windswept rain.

Before he could do anything, the top deck suddenly collapsed beneath the weight of so many people. Hundreds below were crushed by those above. Her structural integrity lost, the next time the *Neptune* rocked to the side, she lacked the balance to right herself again. Capsizing, over a thousand of her passengers were washed into the stormy seas, along with livestock and cargo. She sank rapidly.

Even if there had been time to evacuate ship, the *Neptune* had no lifeboats, no lifejackets and no radios. News of the sinking did not reach Port-au-Prince until 24 hours later, and there wasn't much the military junta could do to help by then anyway. Haiti's barely operative navy was only able to provide two small motorboats to help the rescue efforts. By that point it was too late for most of those who had been on board.

The true number of people who were on the *Neptune* when she capsized is unknown, but was probably well over 2,000. There were 285 survivors, including the captain, who managed to swim to shore using debris to keep himself afloat. Several dozen others also made it to land. Others clung to crates, buckets, bags of coconuts, sacks of charcoal and even dead animals until they were picked up the next day, either by fishing boats or by US Coast Guard ships. The last survivors were picked up two days after the sinking, after which point the USCG crews only found the dead. Some bodies washed up on beaches near where the ferry sank, but most were never found. Fishermen in the area reported a powerful current that may have carried many out to sea, and also prevented all but the strongest swimmers from making it to land.

Haiti's barely operative navy was only able to provide two small motorboats to help the rescue efforts.

Final voyage

As of 2002, the Casamance region's fight for independence from the rest of Senegal had dragged on for 20 years. The western African nation is almost split in two by Gambia, a separate country situated in the middle of Senegal along the banks of the Gambia River. Senegal recognises the independence of Gambia, but not the Casamance region, south of the river, despite Casamance having an ethnic make-up more similar to Gambia or Guinea-Bissau. The separatist fighting made travel across Senegal difficult in the early years of the 21st century, not least because Gambia increased its own security as a response to the trouble along its borders. This led to a big increase in demand for ferries that could take people from Casamance to Dakar, Senegal's capital.

Le Joola had been acquired from Germany by the Senegalese government in 1990. Run by Senegal's military, the 261ft (79.5m) roll-on/roll-off ferry spent her first decade travelling between Casamance and Dakar twice a week. However, she had been out of operation for a year, her port engine being replaced, between 2001 and 2002, so when she was put back into service she only completed the journey once a week whilst her engines were properly run in. This resulted in considerable overcrowding, as happened when she left Ziguinchor in the Casamance region on 26th September.

Le Joola had capacity for 536 passengers, 44 crew and 35 cars. Twice as many people had tickets for this particular journey, with 1,046 having been sold. Labourers and students were her usual passengers, but poor women also used the ferry to reach Dakar so they could sell mangoes and palm oil. The ferry was always overcrowded, but at the end of holidays the numbers trying to get on board always spiked. Plenty of people were allowed aboard without a ticket. Crewmen accepted token kickbacks for pretending they hadn't seen someone board, they let the poorest travel ticketless and without paying out of solidarity, and children under five didn't need a ticket in the first place. En route, *Le Joola* stopped at Carabane, where several hundred more boarded, though nobody knew how many, because the town had no formal port of entry. It was later estimated that she had 1,863 on board when she sank, though some organisations in Senegal speculated there could have been over 2,000.

The ferry left Ziguinchor at 1.30pm. Eyewitnesses on shore later reported that they saw she already had a noticeable list to port. *Le Joola* was only designed to sail in coastal waters. Her flat-bottomed hull (which was necessary to enter shallow waters) offered less resistance against large waves in rough conditions, so she was unsuited to the open sea. In fair conditions she should have been no further than 23 miles (37km) from the coast. At 10pm, when Dakar received their last communication from *Le Joola*, she was 22 miles (35km) off the Gambian coast, and conditions were fine. It was a hot night, and even hotter inside the crowded ferry, so more than a thousand people slept on deck. When she sailed into a freak storm at 11pm, *Le Joola* was top heavy and unstable. Any stability calculations the captain had made before leaving port were now grossly inaccurate.

The storm only lasted a few minutes, but it brought a fierce gale, rough seas and torrential rain. As the ferry rocked, untethered freight slid to the port side, increasing her list. When she began taking on water on the vehicle deck this contributed to the free surface effect. *Le Joola*'s centre of gravity began to shift wildly. The water flooded cabins, caused the ferry's lights to short out, and inspired a mass panic as people tried to escape up on to the top deck, increasing the imbalance and instability even further.

Some survived by climbing onto Le Joola*'s flat hull, where they had to listen to the screaming of those still trapped inside.*

The crew lacked emergency training, and her lifeboats consisted mainly of inadequate inflatable rafts. With no more room on the top deck, people began smashing windows on lower decks to escape through those. Only five minutes after running into trouble, *Le Joola* capsized.

At 7am the next morning, a father showed up at the port in Dakar to collect his four children. They had been travelling alone on *Le Joola*, the eldest being 21. An hour later a police officer told the father that the ferry was running late but would be there soon. Two hours later he was still waiting. He later learnt of what had happened by hearing a radio report. None of his children had survived. It had been their first sea journey.

It was later that morning before government rescue teams reached the site of the disaster, by which time local fishermen had already rescued most of the survivors. The fishermen had to wait until the storm subsided, and whilst over a thousand people on the ferry survived the capsize, many of them didn't survive five hours in the heavy seas. Some survived by climbing onto *Le Joola*'s flat hull, where they had to listen to the screaming of those still trapped inside. The last survivor was a 15-year-old boy, rescued at about 2pm. He confirmed that he had still heard people inside when he was taken off.

Photographs taken from helicopters above the site show the red hull of the capsized ferry barely above the waterline, with an inflatable liferaft floating nearby. *Le Joola* stayed afloat until 3pm, then finally sank, settling in 75ft (23m) of water. There hadn't been time to find a way to release those trapped inside. Divers later retrieved 300 bodies from the wreck. Others washed up on the shore of the Gambian fishing village Tanji.

The public wanted to know why a ship that should have been seaworthy for decades sank after only 12 years in service.

There were only 64 survivors, and only one of them was a woman (despite there being 600 aboard). Throughout Senegal the public outrage and demand from the press led to a public inquiry by the government. The public wanted to know why a ship that should have been seaworthy for decades sank after only 12 years in service. Accusations flew as to whether those running the ferry had only performed as little maintenance on her as they could get away with. The inquiry was closed after only a year, having reached conclusions that were unsatisfying to many. Pay-outs were offered to families of the victims, the Prime Minister and much of her cabinet were sacked, but there were no prosecutions, no formal charges and no legal liability established. The government effectively claimed the disaster was an act of God. It became a political football in Senegal's next elections.

Nationals from many different countries were counted amongst the dead, including numerous African countries,

Lebanon, Spain, Norway, Belgium, the Netherlands and France. As a consequence, the French courts also launched their own inquiry, to the ire of many people in Senegal. It indicted many people at high level for the delay in mounting a rescue that could have saved hundreds more lives.

Beyond a few headlines in the immediate aftermath of the disaster, this was the most attention *Le Joola* received from the Western world. It was certainly more than the *Kiangya*, the *Doña Paz* or the *Neptune* had received. All three recent disasters happened in less developed parts of the world, which lack the stringent regulation of maritime industry as is in place in Europe and the United States. Perhaps, then, these are not major news stories because it is not considered surprising that catastrophes of this magnitude will occur sooner or later. More surprising – and therefore more worthy of headlines – is when ships sink in the West, despite the strictest of safety standards, regardless of loss of life. Only 32 people died when the *Costa Concordia* liner ran aground in January 2012, for example, but it dominated headlines for weeks, precisely because it was so unlikely. It is even more unlikely that a maritime disaster will occur in the West on the scale of *Le Joola*, let alone the *Wilhelm Gustloff*, in the future. The worst maritime disasters will still be happening elsewhere, largely ignored, and quickly forgotten.

INDEX